JUNGIAN REFLECTIONS ON GRANDIOSITY

In *Jungian Reflections on Grandiosity: From Destructive Fantasies to Passions and Purpose,* Francesco Belviso presents a dual view of grandiosity as a destructive obsession that, when approached with curiosity and awareness, has the potential of fueling our lives with a sense of purpose, while being a positive force in the world.

Explaining Jungian psychological concepts in an engaging style, the book begins by examining the origins of grandiose fantasies in children, and how grandiosity persists well into adulthood, in our dreams, fantasies, and strivings. Exploring its relation to narcissism and delusions, the book describes how grandiosity can hijack many areas of our lives—as we chase fame, beauty, knowledge, youth, and even morality—often with disastrous consequences. The book's second half explores how grandiosity can help us identify our passions and callings, ending with a discussion on how to pursue them with integrity and courage. Weaving stories from Greek mythology to Dante's poetry, from the heroic lives of Rosa Parks to Captain Sully, from fairy tales to our everyday decisions about careers, finances, selfies, and dating, and from the lives and nighttime dreams of his patients and his own, Belviso invites us to explore the larger-than-life aspirations that stir us all.

This book offers ideas and tools to better understand our ambitions, challenging us to come to terms with our limitations and find personally meaningful paths forward. *Jungian Reflections on Grandiosity* will be essential reading for academics and students of Jungian studies, as well as analytical psychologists and analysts in practice and in training. It will also be of interest to those wishing to explore Jungian ideas and the role of grandiosity in public and private life.

Francesco Belviso, PhD, PsyD, is an Italian-born psychologist in private practice in Chicago and a lecturer at The C. G. Jung Center of Evanston. He completed his clinical training (Doctoral Internship and Fellowship) at Northwestern University. In his previous professional life, he obtained a doctorate in economics from Princeton University.

"This is a work of alchemy! Dr. Belviso has transformed our concept of grandiosity by revealing the gold in what we most often think of as a pathological symptom. As he decodes the many guises in which grandiosity may appear, we learn that it can be an important and potent fuel in the search for meaning. Engagingly presented using stories of ordinary and not-so-ordinary people, and accessible to a wide variety of readers."—**Robert J. Moretti**, PhD, Associate Clinical Professor of Psychiatry and Behavioral Sciences, Northwestern University Feinberg School of Medicine, and Supervising Analyst, C. G. Jung Institute of Chicago, USA

JUNGIAN REFLECTIONS ON GRANDIOSITY

From Destructive Fantasies to Passions and Purpose

Francesco Belviso

LONDON AND NEW YORK

First published 2020
by Routledge
2 Park Square, Milton Park, Abingdon, Oxon OX14 4RN

and by Routledge
52 Vanderbilt Avenue, New York, NY 10017

Routledge is an imprint of the Taylor & Francis Group, an informa business

© 2020 Francesco Belviso

The right of Francesco Belviso to be identified as author of this work has been asserted by him in accordance with sections 77 and 78 of the Copyright, Designs, and Patents Act 1988.

All rights reserved. No part of this book may be reprinted or reproduced or utilised in any form or by any electronic, mechanical, or other means, now known or hereafter invented, including photocopying and recording, or in any information storage or retrieval system, without permission in writing from the publishers.

Trademark notice: Product or corporate names may be trademarks or registered trademarks, and are used only for identification and explanation without intent to infringe.

British Library Cataloguing-in-Publication Data
A catalogue record for this book is available from the British Library

Library of Congress Cataloging-in-Publication Data
Names: Belviso, Francesco, 1979- author.
Title: Jungian reflections on grandiosity : from destructive fantasies to passions and purpose / Francesco Belviso.
Description: Milton Park, Abingdon, Oxon ; New York, NY : Routledge, 2020. | Includes bibliographical references and index.
Identifiers: LCCN 2019052751 (print) | LCCN 2019052752 (ebook) | ISBN 9780367179380 (hardback) | ISBN 9780367179403 (paperback) | ISBN 9780429058554 (ebook)
Subjects: LCSH: Megalomania. | Jungian psychology. | Psychoanalysis.
Classification: LCC RC553.M43 B45 2020 (print) | LCC RC553.M43 (ebook) | DDC 150.19/54--dc23
LC record available at https://lccn.loc.gov/2019052751
LC ebook record available at https://lccn.loc.gov/2019052752

ISBN: 978-0-367-17938-0 (hbk)
ISBN: 978-0-367-17940-3 (pbk)
ISBN: 978-0-429-05855-4 (ebk)

Typeset in Bembo
by Nova Techset Private Limited, Bengaluru & Chennai, India

To my wife

CONTENTS

Credits	ix
Acknowledgments	xi
Introduction	xiii

PART I
Grandiose fantasies and strivings   **1**

1 What do we seek?	3
2 Grandiosity in children feeds self-esteem and creativity	7
3 We all have "pockets" of grandiosity	17
4 Puer type: Grandiosity unrealized	23
5 Sisyphus type: Grandiosity in action	31

PART II
Everything can be hijacked by grandiosity   **37**

6 Stories of fame, knowledge, and money	39
7 Stories of beauty, youth, perfection—and narcissism	47
8 Stories of altruism, morality, victimhood—and delusions	63

PART III
Callings 75

9 Grandiosity as a calling 77

10 The opposite of grandiosity is laziness 83

11 Ways to identify our grandiosity and callings 91

PART IV
The courage of our insignificance 101

12 The courage to abstain 103

13 The courage to engage 113

14 Wisdom and the acceptance of our insignificance 119

15 The goal is to find gold 129

Index 137

CREDITS

Excerpt from *C. P. Cavafy: Collected Poems* by C. P. Cavafy, translated by Edmund Keeley and Philip Sherrard. Copyright © 1992 by Princeton University Press. Permission conveyed through Copyright Clearance Center, Inc.

CREDITS

Excerpts from C. P. Cavafy, *Collected Poems*, by C. P. Cavafy, translated by Edmund Keeley and Philip Sherrard. Copyright © 1992 by Princeton University Press. Permission conveyed through Copyright Clearance Center, Inc.

ACKNOWLEDGMENTS

I want to thank Stephanie Carrera, Sam Macy, Laura McGrew, Robert Moretti, and Judy Shaw for conversations, feedback on drafts, and encouragement. Judy Shaw suggested the central theme of chapter 10, for which I am grateful. Laura McGrew kindly shared her reflections on the role of conscious doubt in the process of Jungian individuation. Whenever I share stories of patients, I have obtained their permission and asked for feedback on the descriptions of our work together; I thank each of them for their generosity. By changing their identifying information, I have taken all efforts to ensure patients' identities are concealed. I am also grateful to Susannah Frearson—editor at Routledge—who has believed in this project and to Heather Evans for editorial assistance. My wife has been extraordinarily insightful and patient, without her help this book would not have been written—*grazie*.

INTRODUCTION

Donald J. Trump, the 45th president of the United States, once shared the name of his favorite song—"Is That All There Is?" as interpreted by Peggy Lee. In a self-aggrandizing interview, well before his run for the presidency, Trump talked about his alleged successes—a favorite topic of his. Throughout his life, he shared, he would think of this song each time he reached one of his goals, wondering, "Is that all there is?" Then, the central question left unchallenged, he would simply move on to the next thing.[1] The song is hauntingly beautiful, indeed, and Peggy Lee sang it with so much emotion. Each stanza depicts an image in a woman's life. She sings of watching her house being burned down by a majestic fire when she was a child. She describes her first visit to a circus to watch what was advertised as a great show—the best on earth. Lastly, she sings about love found and then lost. Along with the ups and downs, she keeps wondering in a disillusioned, detached way: is that all there is to happiness, and love, and life?

When our plans do not work out as we had hoped, when we face setbacks and losses, we all feel upset and disappointed. Bombarded as we are by images of other people's success, wealth, beauty, and happiness, we may doubt our life choices and self-worth, eaten away by comparisons and impossible standards. Even when we actually accomplish our goals, attaining the milestones we pursued, we may find, perhaps surprisingly, that we do not experience the anticipated sense of relief, happiness, or pride.

We each may be pursuing different goals: a first job, financial success, a romantic relationship, a scientific discovery, a way to be altruistic, a psychological or spiritual insight, an athletic title, a promotion, admission into graduate school, sexual fulfillment, a sense of community, children, or a comfortable retirement. But if we pay attention, we may realize that, as soon as we reach our goals, we quickly start pursuing other ones, more demanding and ambitious than the previous. Driven by big dreams, we are unsure of when we can stop, rest, and call our work completed. Instead, we keep climbing higher and higher, perhaps feeling exhausted along the way or even bored and empty.

Yet, grandiosity—the fantasies and strivings for extraordinary achievements and status—serves an important purpose in our lives. For one, grandiosity fuels the imagination of children and adolescents. Playfully dreaming of grand future accomplishments, children strengthen their identities, self-esteem, and creativity. And these fantasies never entirely disappear in adulthood. Whether hidden in the background of our thoughts or alternatively pursued with all of our energy, they continue to shape our lives for better or worse.

In this book, I explore how grandiosity can result in arrogance, selfishness, and recklessness, hurting not only ourselves but also our loved ones and our communities. Far from focusing only on the pursuit of wealth and fame, I show that grandiosity can hijack any and all areas of our lives, including the ways in which we focus on our physical appearances, pursue knowledge, approach parenting, seek to be moral and altruistic, and even experience our own suffering.

But grandiose fantasies can be helpful too, as they help us discover our passions and callings, the paths that give our lives a sense of purpose. To give up our grandiosity altogether would mean living according to conventions—doing what one is "supposed to do" and what everybody else seems to be doing—which makes it hard to feel alive. The invitation is then to approach our grandiosity with openness and curiosity, and to explore our unique, individual motivations more deeply. Caught between grandiose dreams and inevitable failures, heroic endeavors and ordinary lives, possibilities and hard realities, we are tasked with deciding which pursuits we should engage with and which fantasies are better left behind.

There is nothing new under the sun—as it is written in the book of Ecclesiastes—and this thought accompanied me as I was writing this book. After all, many have investigated grandiosity before, including the author of Ecclesiastes more than two thousand years ago. Among the more recent authors, I closely follow the ideas of the psychoanalysts Carl Jung and Heinz Kohut. I take it as my task to make accessible and jargon-free some of the insights that I have uncovered in my studies and work. My hope is that psychotherapists and other curious readers will find opportunities to gain a deeper understanding of grandiosity in our society, in other people, and most importantly in themselves.

And indeed, we have to approach the topic of grandiosity with caution, as there is the looming temptation to spot the grandiosity in others, rather than in ourselves. The media and our dinner conversations focus, with a gossipy undertone, on the lives of the famous and the wealthy, the boastful and the narcissistic, the successful and the disgraced. "*They* are grandiose, not us," we claim naively. Within the sphere of our personal relationships, we tend to explain other people's behavior as driven by their egocentrism whenever we feel hurt by their—at times legitimate—choices. Popular psychology and self-help books similarly indulge us by offering advice on how to cope with the grandiosity and narcissism of others: our spouses, parents, or bosses. Such advice can be helpful, even lifesaving in abusive relationships, but it may also cloud our capacity for honest self-exploration.[2] We risk using others as screens onto which we project our own grandiosity; what we do not like in ourselves, we readily notice in them.

These days, a formidable hook for our projections is Donald Trump. I remember a patient of mine who openly despised Trump for his showiness and ruthlessness. Yet, my patient had the following nighttime dream: He was excited to be out partying, driven around town in a limo filled with attractive women, all the while taking selfies with Trump. It seems that something in my patient identified with the grandiose lifestyle he was supposedly and emphatically repulsed by. Interestingly, when Trump himself was prodded toward soul-searching, he replied, without irony, that he did not want to think further and analyze himself because he was afraid of what he might discover—about not liking who he is.[3] Surely, Trump has emerged as both an instigator and an expression of the grandiosity of our culture, with its focus on wealth, success, power, and the pursuit of "greatness." And so, it is all the more imperative to strive to understand, contain, and redress our own boundless ambitions, grandiose fantasies, and all-consuming preoccupations—before our communities are ravaged by the sum of them all.

To facilitate this exploration, I share stories that highlight the manifestations and consequences of grandiosity—from the lives of my patients to my own, from mythology to history, from literature to our everyday decisions about finances, selfies, and dating. However, in discussing other people, I do not claim to know the full context or ultimate meaning of their lives and surely am not suggesting any indictment. My hope is that these stories will be seen as opportunities for self-reflection, not judgment.

Lastly, I believe that narratives from these varied sources—including the mythological and literary ones—together with the personal conversations of the psychotherapeutic encounter, provide valuable "data" to shed light on grandiosity. True to how I think through these topics, I will not present statistics or quantitative studies; others have discussed them, reassuringly converging on similar insights.[4] "I absolutely believe in objectivity and in looking at things straight," the psychoanalyst Donald Winnicott once wrote, "but not in making it boring by forgetting the fantasy, the unconscious fantasy."[5]

I wonder if Trump knows that the lyrics of his favorite song—"Is That All There Is?"—were inspired by a short story by Thomas Mann, the German author and Nobel Prize winner for literature. Written in 1896, the story is about a man of unclear age—"he might have been thirty years old, he might have been fifty," as lives unlived seldom leave marks for the passing of time.[6] The man serendipitously approached a stranger in Piazza San Marco in Venice and began an intimate and surreal narration. He shared that everything that had happened in his life—the positive and the negative alike—never truly affected him. As life unfolded in front of his eyes, all he could wonder was, "Is this all there is to it?"[7] Mann's story, titled "Disillusionment," moves into deeper shades of darkness, loneliness, and depression, until the man who could not be moved by his experiences, the man who did not feel alive, dreamt of death itself. Contrary to the song adaptation, however, Mann's character might not have lost all hope. "It is my favorite occupation to gaze at the starry heavens at night," he shared by way of conclusion; "perhaps it may be pardoned in me that I still cling to my distant hopes?"[8] Rather than being swept away by our ambitions, we may wonder if it is possible—and I think it is—to become aware of our grandiosity and harness this energy to enrich our lives and the world with a sense of hope and enthusiasm.

Notes

1. Barbaro, "What Drives Trump?" Barbaro's interview and Trump himself offer rich material on the topic of this book. A Jungian exploration of the Trump phenomenon is Cruz and Buser, *Present Danger*.
2. A tongue-in-cheek cultural exploration of these dynamics is offered by a recent short book aptly titled *The Selfishness of Others: An Essay on the Fear of Narcissism* by Kristin Dombek.
3. Barbaro, "What Drives Trump?"
4. An accessible book on narcissism that is based on contemporary quantitative research and offers a complementary view of grandiosity is Malkin, *Rethinking Narcissism*.
5. Winnicott, *Home*, 205.
6. Mann, "Disillusionment," 23.
7. Mann, "Disillusionment," 25.
8. Mann, "Disillusionment," 27.

References

Barbaro, M. "What Drives Trump? A Fear of Fading Away." *New York Times*, October 25, 2016.
Cruz, L., and S. Buser, ed. *A Clear and Present Danger: Narcissism in the Era of Donald Trump*. Ashville: Chiron Publications, 2016.
Dombek, K. *The Selfishness of Others: An Essay on the Fear of Narcissism*. New York: Farrar, Straus and Giroux, 2016.
Malkin, C. *Rethinking Narcissism: The Secret to Recognizing and Coping with Narcissists*. New York: HarperCollins, 2015.
Mann, T. "Disillusionment." In *Stories of Three Decades*, 23–7. New York: Knopf, 1936.
Winnicott, D. W. *Home Is Where We Start From: Essays by a Psychoanalyst*. London: Pelican Books, 1987.

PART I
Grandiose fantasies and strivings

1
WHAT DO WE SEEK?

A year before he died near the summit of Mount Everest, George Mallory was asked what motivated him to join such dangerous climbing expeditions. Dismissively, he shared that there might be some scientific value to them, adding in jest that "geologists want a stone from the top of Everest." But when Mallory turned more personal, to explain his commitment to summit the highest mountain of the world, he famously quipped, "Because it's there."[1]

And some people may leave it at that. When asked about their lives, they proudly state that they prefer not to complicate things that are meant to be easy. They like to think they know what they want, from their careers to their relationships, and are simply pursuing it. There is nothing deeper influencing their choices, no motivations to be explored, and no fantasies leading them astray. They may even admit that, of course, they are ambitious and competitive, but isn't that what everyone should do—to shoot for the moon?

In my experience, this approach does not work well. Unaware of their motivations, they may have nighttime dreams filled with anxiety and shame: these are caused by the grandiose fantasies that are actually driving them— fantasies more powerful and potentially destructive than they recognize. But when they wake up in the morning, they say it was all just a bad dream, that there is no need to dwell, and that it is funny to observe how silly the brain is. They engage with their days—their work and their families—unaware that those intense preoccupations still reverberate within. And if their superficially-chosen goals turn out to be unfulfilling or their plans come crashing down, they exclaim, "What was I thinking? What did I do with my life?" Their after-the-fact confusion is due to their ignorance of what they were unconsciously seeking. And typically what has not been explored has a tendency to come back out of left field and hit us right on the nose.

Alternatively, we can work to understand our fantasies and motivations. For instance, by paying attention to the ongoing chatter of our minds, we may realize

4 Grandiose fantasies and strivings

that there are certain questions we ask ourselves again and again. These are the questions that motivate us and orient our choices, by which we evaluate our achievements and ourselves. Each of us may focus on very different things—we may "hear" ourselves wondering if we are famous, attractive, knowledgeable, virtuous, altruistic, wealthy, insightful, or worthy of love. In my work as a psychologist and in my own life, I have observed that these questions often share an underlying grandiosity, a preoccupation with extraordinary achievements.

In that same interview, for instance, Mallory further elaborated that climbing Everest was born from the "desire to conquer the universe"—note he did not say explore, but conquer.[2] And even in our most ordinary lives, we may notice that our motivations are just as grandiose. We do not merely question if we are good enough or even better than most. We instead take it a step further, wondering if we are the best—if we are special and unique. We pursue impossible goals. We strive for what may not be in the cards for us. These are the grandiose fantasies that shape our lives.

I once worked with a man in his late thirties who struggled with his dating life. Through online dating, he met several interesting women, happy and hopeful whenever he felt a connection. He was open—with them and me—about his desire for a serious relationship; since his last one ended more than 10 years prior, he had been craving intimacy and partnership. And I, too, was energized by his stories, given his optimism and enthusiasm. Yet, each and every time we spoke, things would come to a sudden stop. Abruptly, his feelings would wane and his struggle would begin. "How is it possible that a woman I liked so much," he would ask me, "all of a sudden does not seem to be a good match for me?" I did not know, and it was puzzling indeed.

A clearer understanding emerged only over time, as he unfortunately went through further cycles of starts and stops—each time causing confusion and pain to both him and his new partners. Luckily, he was able to bring curiosity and honesty to the therapy process, as he agreed to voice out loud his inner dialogues about each relationship. When he met a new potential partner and did not feel a connection, it made sense that he broke it off—in the beginning, there has to be enough interest to pursue things further. But when there was a connection, he finally observed, a question emerged from the inside and imposed itself on him: "Is she the one?"

Now, this is a big question, a question that demands a final yes-or-no answer. But such definite answers are nearly impossible at the beginning of any relationship; it takes time to find out if there is long-term potential. With each new relationship, this question would instead take hold of him and force a decision too early, leading him to withdraw and call things off. These explorations helped my patient discover that he was grandiosely seeking "the perfect partner" and a relationship that knows no doubt—an impossible goal. This realization freed him to evaluate new relationships more humbly, such as asking, "How do I feel when we spend time together? Am I looking forward to meeting again?"

In my own life, I came to realize the importance of inner questions when I started working with terminally ill patients. Years before, I had come to the United States to study at Princeton University, where I graduated with a doctorate in economics. My grandiose fantasies reigned supreme. At the time, I was ambitious and determined to pursue a life in academia. Once established professionally, I thought I might even go into politics. Back then, I was sure that the life trajectory I had pursued would ultimately deliver—together with success and accolades—its promises of contentment and satisfaction. However, that was not the case. I was neither content nor satisfied.

Seeking a doorway into a more purposeful life, and hoping to discover more about myself, I started volunteering in the oncology unit of a hospital in Chicago. Later, I shifted to the more intense experience of home hospice, providing home visits to terminally ill patients. Working in hospice care, I was stunned to notice that those I was assisting rarely talked about their academic degrees, careers, financial successes, the stock market, or the number of bedrooms in their homes. Most people, instead, focused on the people they loved and cared for—both the joys springing from relationships and memories, and the regrets for missed opportunities and lost connections.

One conversation I had the privilege of witnessing was between a terminally ill man, father of two young adults, and his best friend. As the man's health deteriorated and his speech worsened, it became difficult to understand him— when talking requires so much effort, each word becomes precious. His best friend had come for a visit and a goodbye, and he energetically started reassuring my patient. The friend said he would take care of the utility bills, was in contact with the mortgage company, and would help the man's daughter find a summer internship. Clearly, he had already taken care of so many practical things, like a good friend would. For the ill man, who was about to leave his young family behind, such help must have been a godsend. Yet, he wanted to talk about something else. He silenced his friend midsentence and, as we all got closer trying to understand his words, he only said, "I love you."

These experiences shattered my worldview. Until then, I had focused almost exclusively on my academic and career ambitions, at the expense of many other areas. My relationships had suffered the most. I remember myself, as a young adult, wondering which university offered the best doctorate in economics, which city in the world was best to live in, and which next step would be best for my success. My inner dialogues endlessly revolved around these topics, a sad and anxiety-provoking fact that did not register with me back then. It was through my conversations with home hospice patients that I came to notice my inner questions—and it was life-giving for me. I started therapy and began to examine my motivations and goals. A world of curiosity and possibilities opened, including the realization that I found purpose when engaging in questions related to the search for personal meaning. These experiences ultimately led me to become a clinical psychologist.

"Is that all there is?" "Is she the one?" "Which city in the world is best to live in?"—our inner questions have the power of shaping our lives. Left unchecked, these grandiose questions tend to grow into obsessions, impulsive decisions, and impossible pursuits—a recipe for disaster. Hence, we have to become familiar with grandiosity in ourselves and gain some awareness of what we seek. And because grandiosity first emerges in our lives when we are children, this is where our exploration begins.

Notes

1. *New York Times*, "Climbing Mount Everest."
2. *New York Times*, "Climbing Mount Everest."

Reference

New York Times. "Climbing Mount Everest Is Work for Supermen." March 18, 1923.

2
GRANDIOSITY IN CHILDREN FEEDS SELF-ESTEEM AND CREATIVITY

Grandiosity is prevalent among children and adolescents. It is not common for a four-year-old to say, "Look at my drawing, my shapeless scribbles. I think they may be good enough for a kid my age." Most likely, instead, a child who climbs to the top of a jungle gym will scream with excitement, "I did it! Look! I'm champion of the world!" And we hear children and adolescents talk about their future achievements, and how they will become astronauts, the president of the country, rock stars, Olympic athletes, great inventors, and Nobel Prize winners—or possess supernatural powers, like invisibility or the ability to fly. Such musings show up also in children's play and their nighttime dreams. One may judge these common fantasies as silly and without value—the product of children's immature minds. In this chapter, instead, I discuss how these fantasies are not silly; they are actually necessary for children to establish their self-esteem and grow into creative and vital people.

We do not have direct insight into the psychological experiences of infants. It is only when language becomes established, later in life, that we can hear children talk plainly about their thoughts and feelings. Before language, we have to rely on less precise and often less convincing ways to learn about their inner experiences. We can rely on objective, quantitative measures, including registering brain activity or hormonal levels. We can observe in structured ways the interactions between infants and their parents.[1] Alternatively, we can rely on our own empathic imagination—a mix of emotional attunement, curiosity, and introspection that is a favorite method in psychoanalysis.[2]

Starting with Sigmund Freud, psychoanalysts imagined the beginning of children's psychological lives as blissful. When an infant is welcomed into the world by parents who attend to the many physical needs, like food, shelter, and clothing, and who are attuned to the growing emotional needs for soothing and connection, then the infant feels deeply at peace. The child, the caregivers, and the entire world are experienced by the child as one big, reliable, and safe whole. Freud called this blissful state "primary narcissism," which he considered a universal, healthy experience—and different from the most common use of the word "narcissism," a distinction we will explore later.[3]

Other psychoanalysts similarly considered the child's original state as blissful. The British psychoanalyst and pediatrician Donald Winnicott, for instance, wrote about the infant who, when hungry, can simply imagine the breast into existence, meaning that the infant feels that simply wanting something, like food or comfort, is enough for a caregiver to show up and provide it. This illusion is maintained by a caring parent ready to feed the infant whenever there are signs of hunger, or to comfort when distressed, so that no need goes unfulfilled.[4] For the Jungian analyst Erich Neumann, the language swerves toward the poetic when talking about the experience of the infant:

> Nothing is himself; everything is world. The world shelters and nourishes him, while he scarcely wills and acts at all. Doing nothing, lying inert in the unconscious, merely being there in the inexhaustible twilit world, all needs effortlessly supplied by the great nourisher—such is that early, beatific state.[5]

However, all these psychoanalysts recognize that this state of bliss cannot endure for long. Parents cannot remain attuned to the needs of their children all the time, and frustrations to the children's wishes are inevitable.[6] As they grow, children have to accommodate the hard realities of life, including the fact that other people and the world in general cannot satisfy each and every one of their physical and emotional needs or at least not right away. Most children put up a good fight against these realities, as it is hard to leave behind the original blissful state.[7]

One way to describe these transformations is to follow the development of our egos. "Ego" is the Latin word for "I" and, since its introduction in the English translations of Freud, the term has become widely used. The common usage attaches a negative connotation to it. For instance, when we want to indicate that somebody is grandiose, we say, "he has a big ego," betraying our often negative evaluation of those with big ambitions. When psychologists talk about the ego, however, they are referring to something in a person's psychological makeup that is both healthy and needed. In Jungian psychology, the ego is described as the center of consciousness.[8] Possibly more intuitively, we can say that the ego is our sense of identity together with our will—the felt sense that "I" have a certain identity and that "I" live it out with my choices.[9]

From the blissful but naive state of infancy, the ego emerges over time and through experiences. A well-developed ego has the ability to observe fantasies without taking them as objective realities, understand and regulate emotions and desires, relate to other people, sustain self-esteem and focused activity, adapt to and influence the surrounding environment, and cope with the inevitable disappointments and failures. In short, the ego becomes solid as the center of awareness, initiative, and self-esteem, allowing us to gain a sense of mastery over the external world as well as of understanding over our inner lives.

A strong ego, then, does not translate into a boastful personality and is not an expression of narcissism. It is instead an achievement, which makes us feel energized and confident. Conversely, when our self-esteem collapses, we often find ourselves with a deflated ego: we feel irritable, empty, panicky, and indecisive. In his autobiography *Memories, Dreams, Reflections*, the Swiss psychiatrist and psychoanalyst Carl Jung described his realization that a strong ego is necessary to endure and to thrive.

> [It is important to] affirm one's own destiny. In this way we forge an ego that does not break down when incomprehensible things happen; an ego that endures, that endures the truth, and that is capable of coping with the world and with fate. Then, to experience defeat is also to experience victory. Nothing is disturbed—neither inwardly nor outwardly, for one's own continuity has withstood the current of life and of time.[10]

Greek mythology offers an apt description of the challenges we face in establishing a confident ego and a stable sense of identity. The Greek myth of Prometheus, as told by Aeschylus, has its beginning in the so-called Age of Gold, a time when humans and gods lived side by side, sharing meals and libations. In those times, humans did not have to work, as wheat and other vegetables sprouted from the soil and all kinds of meats were provided to them. They did not experience sickness, old age, or death either—they were forever young and blissful.

A terrible fight among the gods—the Olympic gods led by Zeus on one side and Titans on the other—altered this peaceful state and brought the Age of Gold to an end. As the victorious Zeus sat on his throne, the condition of humans dramatically changed. They did not share meals with the gods anymore; hence, the problem of producing their own food arose. They also found themselves vulnerable, threatened by beasts with dangerous claws roaming the earth. Lastly, humans became mortal—they started aging and getting sick. These major changes in their lives were not due to some retribution for having upset the gods. It was merely the result of changing equilibriums among the gods themselves—like a child caught up in a bad divorce.

Luckily, not everyone was unsympathetic to their struggles. Prometheus, a figure of uncertain lineage in between gods and humans, decided to intervene and restore some balance in favor of humanity. He stole fire and the arts of civilization, like farming and metallurgy, from the gods and bestowed them upon humans. With these crucial gifts, humans became able to defend themselves from the wild beasts and cultivate their own food. From being powerless and at the mercy of the gods, humans became confident in their abilities and strengths; this was the birth of their self-esteem.[11]

The Greek myth accurately mirrors the development of the ego. It is indeed a Promethean transformation to grow out of the initial dependency on parents and become an adult capable of fulfilling one's own material wants—a home and a comfortable lifestyle—as well as psychological needs—enjoying relationships and personally meaningful pursuits. And children develop these abilities thanks to their grandiose fantasies and musings—their fragile, nascent egos are strengthened by "stealing" and making their own the attributes of the gods.[12]

When faced by disruptions to the original blissful state, children may become frustrated, scared, or hopeless. Their egos may collapse in shame and their self-esteem tank. It is at those times that grandiose fantasies naturally emerge to reestablish the balance, support the ego, and reclaim some of the lost state of bliss. Children may identify with the comforting and all-powerful qualities of their parents, with the role models exalted in their culture, and with images of perfection, heroism, and grandeur that emerge from their own unconscious—in Jungian parlance, archetypes.[13] These fantasies are not without risks, including the risk of believing in them a bit too much, as will become clear in later chapters.

In the psychological literature, a classic example of disruption to the original blissful state is the arrival of a new sibling. If a little girl has been an only child for a while, she may have mixed feelings about her new family member. The second child dethrones the firstborn, whose special status as the center of the (parents') world is lost. I remember when my neighbor's three-year-old daughter was just about to have a brother. I happened to give her a picture of our cat and later was told that she paraded this picture around for days to all friends and relatives that came to town—relatives who, truthfully, had traveled to see her little brother. The picture had become something special about her that she could offer the adults around her; it was a way to reclaim some of the lost attention.

Grandiose fantasies also allow children to take a step above their current abilities—outside their comfort zone—to take risks, experiment, and be creative. Children may be moved to relive the great adventures of heroes, to explore brand new worlds. Just like seasoned public speakers rehearse their presentations in advance, children can use grandiose fantasies as rehearsal to strengthen their skills and build confidence. They can role-play situations that grown-ups deal with, and they can explore—in fantasy—ways to approach them confidently, without the premature risks of failure and shame.

While some children may use grandiosity to defend against experiences of isolation and loneliness, withdrawing into an internal word of exalted fantasies, grandiosity in most cases fosters relatedness and unites. For instance, children may create shared make-belief scenarios where each child's explorations and ideas enliven the others. Sadly, a cohesive and energized group may express their shared fantasies in ways that are aggressive and destructive toward outsiders. Growing up, one of the ways children in my neighborhood played together was by building amazing devices to throw rocks at imaginary rivals. We would fantasize about the potency of our tools—no need for Freud here—and imagine heroic deeds and our ultimate victory.[14]

Lastly, children who play with grandiose fantasies are imaginatively discovering their potential. Children need to come to believe that their efforts matter and that they can have a positive impact on their lives and the world. The limitations of reality will soon seep in. But in the meantime, they have had an opportunity to open up to possibilities, gain a sense of mastery, and shape the questions that will accompany them for years to come. In summary, grandiosity in childhood is not only common, but needed and healthy. A child who is psychologically free to be grandiose is a child who believes that life can be exciting and enjoyable; a life where accomplishments bring feelings of pride and satisfaction. Conversely, a child who is burdened too early by reality and limitations may not have been touched by the Promethean fire of possibilities.

Parents are crucial to the vicissitudes of children's grandiosity and the emergence of their self-esteem. The psychoanalyst Heinz Kohut argued that the parents' role is to mirror the excitement of the child: "The child needs the gleam in the mother's eye," he famously wrote.[15] Ideally, parents join in with the child, revel in the grandiose ideation without anxiety or a need to quash it, and meet the child with both excitement and pride. Over time, with repeated validating experiences strengthening their egos, children may internalize the source of pride—feeling it alive within themselves. By contrast, children who are neglected or overwhelmed by external circumstances may be hindered in their grandiose imaginings, struggling to develop creativity and self-esteem.

The psychoanalyst Allen Siegel described a playful interaction between a two-year-old child and his father who provided the "just right" participation:

> The boy attempted to stand upright on the palm of his father's outstretched hand. The little boy climbed onto the outstretched palm and, after a short struggle to find his balance, stood straight and tall. The father proudly proclaimed, "Champion of the World!!!" and the boy thrust his arms triumphantly above his head, beaming from ear to ear. Statue-like, they stood united until the boy, knowing just the right moment, turned and jumped into his father's arms as they embraced in a cuddle of delight.[16]

It is important to distinguish this scenario from that of a parent who responds in a generic, distracted, or halfhearted way, commenting only on the most superficial achievements. For instance, a young girl may approach her parent to share about a cool science experiment she did in school, but her parent responds only to the grade she earned on it. It does not matter here if he criticized a low grade or praised a high one—the girl's excitement went unrecognized. Another example would be an "artistic" child who seeks validation for his painting skills, but who can only get praise for his hockey game. The effect of such feedback is that rather than encouraging children to be themselves, they are pushed to comply with the values of their parents—to perform in order to be noticed. Kohut argued that such children may be left forever dependent on the parents—or some other audience—to receive their intensely needed validation. For these children, grandiosity may persist without transforming into self-esteem, creativity, and enjoyment. In fact, we cannot enjoy our achievements if we are required to succeed in areas we do not personally value as important. While parents will not get it right every time, "good enough" parenting includes ample opportunities for accurate mirroring and felt excitement.

Some may argue that parents should not validate their children "too much," lest children grow up with unrealistic assessments of their own skills and worth. Parents who constantly praise their children and over-protect them from disappointment, it is argued, end up bringing forth vulnerable, entitled, and self-centered adults. Much of our current narrative about the Millennials revolves around these themes. However, no matter how much praise a child receives from parents and educators, the realities of life will sooner or later challenge feelings of specialness and grandiosity. Nobody, no matter how sheltered, can escape this reckoning. At some point, children will participate in a race with friends, only to find they cannot win. They will not be chosen by the teacher to complete a task. A busy parent may not be able to enthusiastically comment on their latest Lego creations. Each of these small injuries to the children's egos is what we may call "reality seeping in." Children's own limitations, as well as those of the people around them, serve as a reality-check to their grandiose fantasies.

Parents continue to have a role here, which is to soften the blow. These episodes of disillusionment should be gradual, lest children's overall sense of worth be shattered. And because children see their parents as "god-like," as Kohut wrote, parents can restore the lost balance and strength with soothing words.[17] Here again, psychology and Greek mythology mirror one another—Prometheus softened the blow by supporting and strengthening humans.

We return to the story quoted previously of the "Champion of the World" child, lifted up in glorious excitement by his father. The psychoanalyst Siegel witnessed another interaction between the same father-and-son couple, this time when they were together on a military airbase:

> As we walked through the massive building a jet turned onto the runway directly in front of us. The noise was deafening. The ground shook and the air distorted as waves of heat rose from the roaring engines. It was a frightening experience for us all. In a matter of seconds "Champion of the World" had melted into a puddle of terrified tears and the same hand that supported his mighty exhibitionism now scooped him up and held him in a different sort of embrace. No cuddle of delight, this embrace recognized and accepted "Champ's" terror and supported "Champ's" vulnerability with the same strength that had earlier supported his expansiveness.[18]

If their confidence is not shattered too quickly and injuries to their egos are not too crushing, then growing children will be able to absorb the feedback and revise their grandiose self-image toward more realistic and accurate views of themselves—until a time when, having become adults able to sustain a stable sense of self-esteem and vitality, they can let go of their grandiose fantasies and preoccupations. Psychological development, however, never follows this neat linear progression. Regardless of the quality of parenting they received, most people continue to harbor grandiose fantasies throughout their lives. And while grandiosity can remain enlivening in adulthood too, it can just as easily set us on impossible and dangerous paths, wreaking havoc in our lives.

Hinting to the ever-present destructive potential of grandiosity, Prometheus remains an ambiguous figure in Greek mythology. His actions elevated humans toward the gods—and perhaps too high—letting them access mighty and dangerous powers. For his actions, Prometheus was severely punished by Zeus. He was bound by chains to a column, suspended between earth and sky, with his liver devoured by eagles—an image that cautions against the risks of unbridled grandiosity.

Notes

1. By "parents," I mean any person who interacts with the infant on a regular basis. The more inclusive word "caregiver" would not work: some caregivers cannot give care. The etymology of parent is "to give birth," but also "to bring forth" the infant into the world; it is to this latter meaning that I am referring.
2. The psychoanalyst Heinz Kohut most clearly spoke of the use of empathy to learn about the inner experiences of infants (as well as adults), but he also warned us about the limitations of such an approach. "The psychoanalytic formulation of early experience is difficult and fraught with danger," Kohut wrote. "The reliability of our empathy, a major instrument of psychoanalytic observation, declines the more dissimilar the observed is to the observer, and the early stages of mental development are thus, in particular, a challenge to our ability to empathize with ourselves, i.e., with our own past mental organizations." Kohut, *Analysis of the Self*, 37. A similar criticism—that we may project our own fantasies on infants' experiences—can apply also to archetypal psychological approaches, such as that of Erich Neumann, where mythological stories are taken to elucidate psychological experiences from infancy to adulthood and beyond. A critique of Erich Neumann's approach is Giegerich, "Ontogeny = Phylogeny?"
3. Sigmund Freud, "On Narcissism: An Introduction."
4. Winnicott, *Family and Individual Development*.
5. Neumann, *History of Consciousness*, 15.
6. The memory of an original blissful state may be present even when the experiences in childhood were not been blissful at all due to early losses, trauma, privations, or parents who were unable to care. We often seem to idealize the good old days—real or wished for—of care and innocence. For obvious reasons, the challenges of moving into adulthood and strengthening the ego can be much harder if childhood did not provide safety and manageable opportunities for growth.
7. Some psychoanalysts, including Freud, argued that we must completely leave behind these illusions of infancy. At best, in his view, the original sense of bliss transforms into nostalgia for our childhood. Even more, Freud argued that all illusions should be given up: accepting the hard facts of life is all that matters. Others, including Kohut and Jung, felt that some of those early feelings of completeness and bliss can transform in adulthood and have the function of invigorating our lives with energy and a sense of purpose.

8. Jung, *Psychological Types*, 425.
9. The psychoanalytic concept of the ego has been reinterpreted and modified over the years, also in light of findings in neuropsychology. The Jungian analyst Marcus West offers a model of the ego that distinguishes a person's *sense of being*—determined by affective experiences, such as pleasure, anger, liking—and the *sense of "I"*—a broader, "from above" sense of identity that frames and observes current experiences. Following the work of Melanie Klein, he argues that the sense of being is present since birth, a nonverbal experience of self and the world surrounding infants, an experience that may be more fragmented than blissful. The sense of "I," instead, is a later verbal emergence in children's development. It emerges due to the integration of experiences, including those that are frustrating and disappointing, and its development loosely follows the lines indicated in this chapter with respect to the development of the ego. For a comprehensive review of the history of the concept of the ego and for an exposition of West's affect-identity model, see West, *Feeling, Being, and Self*, chapter 2.
10. Jung, *Memories, Dreams, Reflections*, 297.
11. Another myth that depicts the loss of the original blissful state is the expulsion from the Garden of Eden, that place where everything was provided to humans. In this myth, it is humans that initiate change, by "overreaching" and eating from the tree of knowledge of good and evil. The result of their action was that their conscious, adult lives began: these first humans became aware of the realities of life, including the need for work, of the existence of pain, and of their mortality. For a psychological interpretation of this Biblical story, see chapter 12, and also Jacoby, *Longing for Paradise*, part 2, chapter 14 and Edinger, *Ego and Archetype*, chapter 1.
12. Jung did not write much about the development of the ego—he was mostly focused on adults, especially the challenges pertaining to the "second half" of life—but other Jungian analysts did explore childhood, including Michael Fordham and Neumann. An introduction and overview of Fordham's work is Astor, *Michael Fordham*. Neumann's monumental work on ego development is presented in his *History of Consciousness* as well as *The Child*. A more approachable book that builds on Neumann's ideas is Edinger, *Ego and Archetype*. A review of the Jungian psychology's approach to child development is Main, *Childhood Re-imagined*.

    Kohut directly explored how grandiose fantasies help establish self-esteem. While I do not offer in this book an exhaustive presentation of his ideas, it is worth mentioning that when discussing the typical development out of primary narcissism, Kohut distinguished between two separate aspects. The first he called the "idealized parental imago," occurring when the child attaches ideas of perfection to his parents or other figures in his life. By associating with these exalted figures, the child can restore some of the lost original bliss. Over time, the gradual withdrawing of these projections of perfection gives rise to the formation of one's own ideals. The other aspect is the "grandiose self," describing how the child attaches fantasies of grandiosity, perfection, and omnipotence to her own self. If parents respond positively to these fantasies, Kohut argued, the grandiose self transforms into a child's (realistic) ambitions. One's ideal and ambitions, then, emerge from separate attempts to cope with the loss of the original blissful state. See Kohut, *Analysis of the Self*, as well as his *Restoration of the Self*. An excellent review of Kohut's ideas is Siegel, *Kohut*. I do not find Kohut's distinction between grandiose self and idealized parental imago crucial for my explorations; hence, I do not pursue it further. The interested reader can learn more about the similarities and differences among Kohutian and Jungian approaches in Jacoby, *Individuation and Narcissism*.

13. For instance, when discussing the frequent crushes adolescents experience toward older people of all genders, the Jungian psychoanalyst Marie-Louise von Franz wrote, "The natural reaction of the young admirer is that he would like to be like the object of his admiration. So the figure functions as a model of a more adult way of existence or behavior. It is a projection of the Self. As long as the ego complex is weak, this projection functions as a model to be copied and followed. It assists in building up a more adult ego complex. ... You can say that the ego has an archetypal foundation, and it is the Self which builds up the ego complex. It is this aspect that is meant by the hero or heroine of a fairy tale: the archetypal foundation of an individual ego." *Feminine in Fairy Tales*, 20. A sustained identification with these archetypal characters in adulthood, however, is problematic—one ends up thinking that he is God's gift to humanity... if not God himself. I will discuss these processes of inflation in chapter 8.
14. The contagious, collective effects of grandiosity can have disastrous consequences, all the way to causing political aberrations and wars.
15. Kohut, "Forms and Transformations of Narcissism," in Morrison, *Essential Papers on Narcissism*, 69.
16. Siegel, *Kohut*, 87.
17. See Siegel, *Kohut*, 42.
18. Siegel, *Kohut*, 87.

References

Astor, J. *Michael Fordham: Innovations in Analytical Psychology*. London: Routledge, 1995.

Edinger, E. *Ego and Archetype: Individuation and the Religious Function of the Psyche*. New York: Putnam, 1972.

Freud, S. "On narcissism: An introduction." In *The Standard Edition of the Complete Psychological Works of Sigmund Freud*, edited and translated by J. Strachey. Vol. 14:67–102. New York: W. W. Norton, 1981. First published 1914.

Giegerich, W. "Ontogeny = Phylogeny? A Fundamental Critique of Erich Neumann's Analytical Psychology." *Spring* 1975, 75.

Jacoby, M. *Longing for Paradise: Psychological Perspectives on an Archetype*. Toronto: Inner City Books, 2006.

Jacoby, M. *Individuation and Narcissism: The Psychology of Self in Jung and Kohut*. Oxford: Routledge, 2017. First published 1990.

Jung, C. G. *Psychological Types*. Vol. 6 of *The Collected Works of C. G. Jung*, edited by H. Read, M. Fordham, G. Adler, and W. McGuire. Translated by R. F. C. Hull. Princeton, NJ: Princeton University Press, 1971.

Jung, C. G. *Memories, Dreams, Reflections*. New York: Random House, 1989. First published 1961.

Kohut, H. *Analysis of the Self: A Systematic Approach to the Psychoanalytic Treatment of Narcissistic Personality Disorders*. Chicago: University of Chicago Press, 2009. First published 1971.

Kohut, H. *The Restoration of the Self*. Chicago: The University of Chicago Press, 2009. First published 1977.

Main, S. *Childhood Re-imagined: Images and Narratives of Development in Analytical Psychology*. East Sussex: Routledge, 2008.

Morrison, A. P., ed. *Essential Papers on Narcissism*. New York: New York University Press, 1986.

Neumann, E. *The Origins and History of Consciousness.* Princeton: Princeton University Press, 2014. First published 1970.

Neumann, E. *The Child: Structure and Dynamics of the Nascent Personality.* Oxford: Routledge, 2018. First published 1973.

Siegel, A. M. *Heinz Kohut and the Psychology of the Self.* Hove, England: Brunner-Routledge, 1996.

von Franz, M-L. *The Feminine in Fairy Tales.* Boulder, Colorado: Shambhala, 1993.

West, M. *Feeling, Being, and the Sense of Self.* London: Karnac, 2007.

Winnicott, D. W. *The Family and Individual Development.* Oxon: Routledge, 1964. First published 2006.

3
WE ALL HAVE "POCKETS" OF GRANDIOSITY

The grandiose imaginings of children evolve over time. Leaving behind their exaggerated ambitions, growing children tend to sober up and mature into choosing attainable goals. They become able to evaluate more accurately their abilities and take into account their limitations. They hopefully gain a solid grasp on reality, adapting to their life circumstances. But grandiose fantasies never completely disappear.

For one, childhood grandiosity may survive by morphing into the ambitions and ideals of adults.[1] If we trace our current passions back in time—whether they are social activism, a desire for professional success, or an interest in the arts—we most likely recognize that they began all the way back in our childhood; our childhood musings and fixations often are the seeds of our adult interests. And some of our early grandiosity persists well into adulthood without evolving much, carrying the same rambunctious strength of our early years. These are our enduring fantasies of accomplishing deeds and achieving status that are above, beyond, and outside the bounds of ordinary existence. For most of us, these are not immediately apparent; if someone asks us about our life goals, or if we wonder about our ambitions, we may not think to acknowledge these fantasies. Yet, they continue to influence our motivations and choices.

These grandiose preoccupations live in "pockets" within us; pockets into which, from time to time, we may unwittingly fall. Especially at times of transition, these grandiose fantasies are reactivated, ushered in by the excited feelings evoked by success, like a promotion or a long-sought big break; new beginnings, like a career change or moving to a new city; and even endings, like being fired or a divorce. In fact, even difficult experiences can open up the possibility of new beginnings, with the related fantasies of how our lives may radically change. And once grandiosity is active in us, swept away by its intensity, we are more likely to make decisions that are impulsive and risky, if not completely ill-conceived. Hence, we have to get to know these pockets, to explore their contents with curiosity and honesty.

If we are to look for grandiosity within ourselves, however, we may find the definition offered previously extreme—achievements outside the bounds of ordinary existence, a desire to be the best—the champion of the whole world! It would be a (tempting) mistake to infer that this definition only describes those people who, struggling with a biologically-driven psychiatric disorder or a drug-induced high, may end up thinking they are literally Jesus, an international rock star, or some other famous person. Instead, the desire to be extraordinary is more common in healthy adults than one may think.

The reason why we can be grandiose and sane at the same time is that we usually refashion these intense aspirations into a more manageable frame, so that our goals appear reasonable and attainable. Underneath, however, we are animated by fantasies, passions, and obsessions that are just as wild as they were in childhood.

For instance, we may narrow down our aspirations to specific areas worth pursuing—fame, morality, beauty, wealth, or knowledge, to name just a few—while dismissing all other values and goals as irrelevant, superficial, or vain. We may elevate our careers or fields of study above all others. We may glorify our sought-after accomplishments, from official recognitions to career milestones, as the only ones worthy of praise—forgetting that the casual observer may not find them to be impressive or even relevant. Academicians endlessly talk about their books or grants. Law students gloat for making the law review. Beauty pageant contestants proudly share about their state finals. Runners preach about the beauty of long runs. Children are boastful when they graduate to a purple belt in martial arts. But how many of us know the order of belt colors?

To accommodate reality, we also elect more manageable reference groups for our enduring grandiose fantasies. Rather than comparing herself with Steve Jobs, a businesswoman may compare herself with other entrepreneurs in town and strive to be the most successful. Rather than comparing himself with a saint, a man may take pride in being the most generous alumnus of his college class. Rather than comparing herself with the latest top model, a woman may strive to affirm her superior beauty within her circle of friends. The intensity of our grandiosity does not change based on the size of the chosen reference group.

And grandiosity indeed thrives on comparisons to other people. Regardless of what specifically motivates us—extreme generosity or unapologetic selfishness, spiritual concerns or material possessions, virtues or entitlement—grandiosity seeks to establish each of us as unique and special. And to feel accomplished at all, we need to be "more" than everyone else; we have to be the best. These are the strict comparisons and standards by which we judge ourselves, making it impossible to accept the idea of being ordinary, "good enough," or like everyone else.

In short, we cleverly choose a smaller world in which to measure ourselves and then strive to be the champion of *that* world. The little prince—the protagonist of the eponymous book by Antoine de Saint-Exupéry—travels from planet to planet, until he arrives on a small planet with just one inhabitant, a boastful, conceited man, who likes to assume that everyone admires him.

> "Do you really admire me very much?" he demanded of the little prince.
> "What does that mean—'admire'?"
> "To admire means that you regard me as the handsomest, the best-dressed, the richest, and the most intelligent man on this planet."
> "But you are the only man on your planet!"
> "Do me this kindness. Admire me just the same."[2]

Bored with the conversation, the little prince decides to depart, leaving the boastful man alone with his extraordinary achievements on his empty planet.

When grandiosity is activated, it becomes our driving force and commands all of our energy. We may be consumed with ruminating, scheming, and planning ways to achieve our goals. Depending on the focus of our grandiose preoccupations, we may doggedly work while dismissing other activities, including idle time, as unproductive and irrelevant. We may not value time spent with loved ones. Or we may stop attending to the requirements of our jobs and lose track of our finances. This intense, narrow focus on achieving may appear to the outside observer as an obsession (if mostly played out in our fantasies) or as a compulsion (if it leads to goal-oriented activities).

Contrary to what is commonly assumed, grandiosity does not necessarily translate into being showy or boastful. For some, the drive toward extraordinary achievements is lived as a very private experience. The privacy of the experience itself can become an expression of the specialness of the person. Those pursuing some versions of transcendence or enlightenment, for instance, may harbor private feelings of being "spiritually superior" or having access to unique knowledge and insight. Just as private is the inner conversation of a struggling adolescent who thinks "nobody gets me" or "nobody will ever love me." These thoughts may not seem grandiose; after all, they highlight "negative" qualities and suggest a deflated self-esteem. However, they also contain the idea of being special and unique—the most misunderstood, the most unlovable. Rather than accepting the sad reality that misunderstandings happen and love is not always reciprocated, adolescents may escape these painful realizations by identifying with the figure of the outcast, deriving some pride from feeling rejected—at least until the opportunity to return to relatedness arises.

For some people, grandiose fantasies may be accompanied by feelings of anxiety and restlessness. Others may feel empty, or even bored with their circumstances, waiting for their grandiose vision of life to finally arrive. Whenever negative feedback, a perceived failure, or a stumbling block appears, people may experience intense disillusionment. Then, periods of negative self-evaluations and

20 Grandiose fantasies and strivings

feelings of inadequacy burst through, sometimes with shame, sometimes with rage. While these experiences can be worrisome, they are not uncommon. Lastly, many people driven by grandiosity may not experience any of these unsettling feelings. They may be focused or noncommittal, reserved or boastful, industrious or contemplative, but they all feel energized and stimulated by their grandiose fantasies and pursuits.

Grandiose preoccupations are accompanied by elaborate fantasies as to what reaching our ultimate goals will bring into our lives. When we succeed—it is hoped—there will finally be a sense of pride, peace, exuberance, happiness, and spontaneity. Under the spell of grandiosity, we may think that extraordinary achievements will grant us access to the Mount Olympus of the gods, where we are not touched anymore by the offenses of ordinariness and reality, where we can exist beyond needs and vulnerability. Until then, we give up the desire to feel content and satisfied—these feelings are on hold until our grandiose tasks are achieved.

Following an unexpected layoff, a young man found himself struggling financially and needing to borrow some money from his siblings, a necessity which brought much shame. Finally, having persisted in his job search, he found a new job—a good job, comparable to his last one. Within a few months, he was able to repay his debt and get his career back on track. However, all he could now notice was that his same-paygrade peers were five to ten years younger than him. Filled again with shame and comparisons, his self-esteem tanked. Forgetting that he had just avoided a disaster and that his skills had landed him a job so quickly, he instead returned to his usual concerns: without bigger and bigger successes, his life would amount to little. When caught by grandiose strivings, we do not appreciate our accomplishments, devalue the skills and hard work they required, and quickly forget all the obstacles that we overcame. Grandiosity can only look toward an imagined future; the lived past is already taken for granted, when maybe it should not be.

And so, people driven by grandiose fantasies never seem to reach their goals. The businessman Bill Gates shared a list of favorite books with *The New York Times*. He said that he loved *The Great Gatsby* by F. Scott Fitzgerald, the American classic.[3] He reread it several times and even painted a quote from the book on a wall—in his 2,100-square-foot home library: "His dream must have seemed so close that he could hardly fail to grasp it." Fitzgerald, however, was caught mid-sentence. The quote in its entirety is as follows:

> His dream must have seemed so close that he could hardly fail to grasp it. He did not know that it was already behind him, somewhere back in that vast obscurity beyond the city, where the dark fields of the republic rolled on under the night.
>
> Gatsby believed in the green light, the orgiastic future that year by year recedes before us. It eluded us then, but that's no matter—tomorrow we will run faster, stretch out our arms farther. ... And one fine morning—[4]

Not reaching the goals of our grandiose fantasies is not necessarily for lack of trying, often neither for lack of luck. Simply, it is because the sought-after green light of Gatsbyan memory recedes after all. As soon as one goal is achieved, we quickly replace it with new goals and new horizons. Maybe this is how we protect ourselves from the realization that the project of grandiosity could be flawed and that the bliss of Olympus may be inaccessible after all.

Notes

1. Heinz Kohut, "Forms and Transformations of Narcissism," in Morrison, *Essential Papers on Narcissism*, 64–73. An excellent review of Kohut's ideas is Siegel, *Kohut*.
2. de Saint-Exupéry, *The Little Prince*, 40.
3. Gates, "My 10 Favorite Books."
4. Fitzgerald, *The Great Gatsby*, 182. Ellipsis in the original.

References

de Saint-Exupéry, A. *The Little Prince. Translated by Katherine Woods*. New York: Harcourt Brace & Company, 1943.
Fitzgerald, F. S. *The Great Gatsby*. New York: Scribner, 1925.
Gates, B. "My 10 Favorite Books: Bill Gates." *New York Times Styles Magazine*, May 20, 2016.
Morrison, A. P., ed. *Essential Papers on Narcissism*. New York: New York University Press, 1986.
Siegel, A. M. *Heinz Kohut and the Psychology of the Self*. Hove, England: Brunner-Routledge, 1996.

4

PUER TYPE

Grandiosity unrealized

In our discussion thus far, there has been some ambiguity on whether grandiosity mainly affects people's thoughts and fantasies, or instead if it shows primarily in their actions. To explore how grandiosity influences our lives, it is valuable to make this distinction sharp by describing two psychological types, two ways people live out their grandiosity. I am well aware of the limitations of such generalizations, as everyone's experiences are unique and do not fall neatly into separate categories. My hope is that by introducing the idea of types and providing alternative examples of grandiosity, we can better reflect on how it manifests in ourselves. In this chapter, I discuss those characterized as "Puer types," for whom grandiosity presents only in fantasies, including in the stories that they tell about themselves. By way of contrast, I call "Sisyphus types" those who put their grandiosity into action and, for better or worse, actually pursue their goals; I discuss the latter in the next chapter.

Puer Aeternus is Latin for the forever child. It is one of the names of the child-god Iacchus, as mentioned in Ovid's *Metamorphoses*, who has the semblance of a boy and never grows up into an adult.[1] This imagery was also used for depicting Dionysus and the popular representation of Cupid as a winged child shooting arrows. A more recent personification of the child who never grows up is the story of Peter Pan. The psychoanalysts Carl Jung and Marie-Louise von Franz presented the *Puer Aeternus*, or simply *Puer*, as a type in their theory of psychological development; it is on their work that this chapter builds.[2]

What characterizes Puer types is a stubborn determination not to become adults; that is, a resistance to move from the psychology of the child to the responsibilities, challenges, and gratifications that are unique to adulthood. It is a timely concept, as the youth of recent generations increasingly need more transitional years before they can establish themselves as adults. Young people even adopted a new verb—"to adult"—to describe the efforts of attending to their

24 Grandiose fantasies and strivings

growing responsibilities, as in "I paid rent. I must be adulting." Meanwhile, psychologists have proposed the introduction of yet another intermediate stage, called "emerging adulthood," a label that betrays our desire to soften the blow of becoming (simply, without qualifiers) adults.

It is true, however, that it is not easy to become adults, especially in our complex society. While each life trajectory is different, many young people face common challenges such as leaving their parents' homes, navigating serious romantic relationships, establishing new friendships, and probably the most "adult" task of all, starting their careers. If they embrace these adventures in earnest—a feat that requires courage and strength—they are affected on two levels. Outwardly, they open themselves up to experiencing successes but also rejections and failures. Inwardly, they begin to develop new psychological skills and adaptations; they become more resilient and able to face disappointments without major blows to their self-esteem. Ultimately, as they navigate these transitions, young people become able to stand on their own feet intellectually, emotionally, and financially. They are empowered to shape the trajectory of their lives.

People who live out the psychology of Puer types, instead, resist these transformations. They would rather extend the period of adolescence indefinitely, regardless of their actual ages. von Franz offered a tongue-in-cheek account of a typical day in the life of a Puer type. Her description reminds me of the summer days of my adolescence when the school year was finally over and we were able to enjoy idle time for a few months. But, in her vignette, von Franz was talking about much older adults:

> He gets up at 10:30 a.m., hangs around till lunch time with a cigarette in his mouth, giving way to his emotions and fantasies. In the afternoon he means to do some work but first goes out with friends and then with a girl, and the evening is spent in long discussion about the meaning of life. He then goes to bed at one, and the next day is a repetition of the one before.[3]

Observed from the outside, Puer types do not fully engage with their lives. They may rely—well into adulthood—on their parents, a prolonged dependency that may be both financial and emotional. Instead of committing to a romantic relationship, they may be eager to meet ever new partners. Similarly, they may not want to commit to jobs, much less focus on long-term careers. Puer types live keeping all doors open and trying out possibilities endlessly.

Psychologically, Puer types' driving force is the desire to avoid confrontations with the limitations of reality. To enter adult life means to commit, to stand by one's convictions and decisions. But if Puer types were to commit to people, a career, or a course of action, then they would become vulnerable to experiencing failure. If they took a step in one direction, then they would have to stick around to see the outcome: maybe it works, maybe it does not. Romantic partners may break up with them. They may struggle to get into their graduate schools of choice. They may be passed over for promotion at work. These are all unfortunate but possible outcomes, which are due to a combination of chance, circumstance, and also plain mistakes.

Seeking protections from life's challenges, Puer types may look for a strategy to spare themselves the bitter taste of failure, while artificially sustaining their self-esteem. Grandiosity may be just such a strategy. As discussed earlier, grandiosity is common and healthy among children. For children, it creates a mental space where they can experiment with possibilities and choices in their imagination, without the risks of premature failure and shame. These grandiose fantasies fuel children's self-esteem and psychological growth; grandiosity makes it possible to start putting into action their ambitions and dreams.

Puer types, instead, maintain the grandiose fantasy life of their adolescence unchanged well into adulthood. For them, these early fantasies are never transformed to accommodate reality, and their ambitions are not put into feasible plans. Nothing is ever actively and concretely pursued. Puer types may fancy becoming writers, discovering some new physical properties of the world, or becoming successful politicians—possibly all of these at once—without taking steps in any chosen direction. Fiction becomes the only reality in their lives. And in the work of fiction *The Great Gatsby*, we find a most vivid account of grandiose fantasies in the psychology of a Puer type, in this case of Jay Gatsby—who was actually called James Gatz until he decided to change his name:

> He had changed it at the age of seventeen and at the specific moment that witnessed the beginning of his career ... I suppose he'd had the name ready for a long time, even then. His parents were shiftless and unsuccessful farm people—his imagination had never really accepted them as his parents at all. The truth was that Jay Gatsby, of West Egg, Long Island, sprang from his Platonic conception of himself. [That is, from his own idealized form, his grandiose fantasy.] He was a son of God ... he invented just the sort of Jay Gatsby that a seventeen-year-old boy would be likely to invent, and to this conception he was faithful to the end.
>
> But his heart was in a constant, turbulent riot. The most grotesque and fantastic conceits haunted him in his bed at night. ... Each night he added to the pattern of his fancies until drowsiness closed down upon some vivid scene with an oblivious embrace. For a while these reveries provided an outlet for his imagination; they were a satisfactory hint of the unreality of reality, a promise that the rock of the world was founded securely on a fairy's wing.[4]

Puer types seek instant gratification. For instance, their grandiosity may show as regularly buying lottery tickets while having elaborate ideas of what their lives would be if they won—these reveries being the gratification. Or they may spend much time thinking of a new phone "app" that is going to make them rich, not considering that a good idea would need to be transformed into a business company, a feat that requires lots of work. In general, Puer types dismiss endeavors that require patience, consistency, tenacity, and learning, especially learning through repetition. It is a considerable psychological development when we accept that we have to work hard for our accomplishments, and that fantasies of immediate success have to be sacrificed so that we can learn new skills. For instance, we have to accept spending hours practicing piano, math, or soccer before we can do any of them well—there are no shortcuts.

Similarly, Puer types may resist what they consider the stifled, bourgeois approach to work: the corporate life, the nine-to-five, and any and all jobs that are not seen as creative. A patient of mine, who was struggling to hold a job, exclaimed: "The cubicle is literally a coffin!" And yet, it is a humbling experience to wake up in the morning, on a cold and rainy day, and go do our job, even if we would prefer not to. The story of "Bartleby the Scrivener" comes to mind, a short story written in 1853 by Herman Melville. Bartleby is employed as a clerk in a Wall Street law office. Suddenly, and for the rest of his life, whenever asked to do something for his employer, he refuses. "I would prefer not to," he politely answers back with no further explanation; he just sits idle at his desk. The rejection of the world of duties is absolute. I hope I am not giving Puer types any ideas here: Melville's story does not end well for Bartleby.

Online dating platforms undoubtedly feed into the adolescent psychology of Puer types. Rather than committing to a partner and navigating the inevitable disillusionment and conflicts, these platforms create the illusion of having an endless pool of possibilities. I have met young adults who schedule new dates with strangers on the same day they break up with their partners. Others reach out to new people, even after having met somebody they are genuinely interested in, just to maximize their odds. Everyone is in a rush, and there is no time for sadness or disappointment, or even merely patience, to see where things go. The revolving door of flings and relationships provides Puer types with insurance against the possibility of being hurt.

The refusal of the world of responsibilities and commitments is so central in *The Little Prince* by the French author Antoine de Saint-Exupéry, that the psychoanalyst von Franz interpreted this celebrated childhood story as a manifesto of Puer types.[5] de Saint-Exupéry argued for the value of upholding one's own specialness, creativity, and sensitivity. He seemed to think that adulthood inevitably brings death to dreams and imagination. For instance, he contrasted the virtues and grandiose fantasies of childhood with a cartoonish characterization of the world of adults:

> After some work with a colored pencil I succeeded in making my first drawing. ... The grown-ups' response, this time, was to advise me to ... devote myself instead to geography, history, arithmetic and grammar. That is why, at the age of six, I gave up what might have been a magnificent career as a painter. ... In the course of this life I have had a great many encounters with a great many people who have been concerned with matters of consequence. ... I have seen them intimately, close at hand. And that hasn't much improved my opinion of them.

> Whenever I met one of them who seemed to me at all clearsighted, I tried the experiment of showing him my drawing ... I would try to find out, so, if this was a person of true understanding. ... [After feeling misunderstood by the grown-up's response,] I would bring myself down to his level. I would talk to him about bridge, and golf, and politics, and neckties. And the grown-up would be greatly pleased to have met such a sensible man.[6]

It is too partial a worldview to reduce the totality of adult life—with its passions, sacrifices, successes, and failures—to only its most vain and empty aspects, such as the pursuit of money and status: bridge, golf, and neckties. In the story, de Saint-Exupéry was happy to meet a child, the little prince, who finally understood him. As they reflected together on life and its meaning, they denounced adulthood and its preoccupations, while reclaiming the right to remain in the naive "perfection" of childhood. But every worldview has its consequences, and *The Little Prince* ends with a nostalgic tone and an unfulfilled wish.

Puer types may be stuck in what the psychoanalyst H. G. Baynes called the "provisional life," the sense that they are not yet living their real lives. When the conditions are right—possibly when their big break materializes—only then will they enter the flow of life, so that their true nature will be revealed for all to see. As von Franz wrote,

> There is often, to a smaller or greater extent, a savior complex, or a Messiah complex, with the secret thought that one day one will be able to save the world; the last word in philosophy, or religion, or politics, or art, or something else, will be found. This can go so far as to the typical pathological megalomania, or there may be minor traces of it in the idea that one's time "has not yet come."[7]

For the time being, dabbling in this and that, Puer types are just waiting. They may not experience their provisional lives as problematic, as grandiose fantasies of special status and future successes sustain their self-esteem, at least for a while. But reality has a stubborn way of making itself known, and Puer types may be forced to reckon with the demands of adult life, first among them the need to work and earn a living. This reckoning is a process that may crush their spirits and imperil their wobbly self-esteem.

Feeling threatened by reality, Puer types' flight into fantasy and grandiosity may increase over time. A vicious circle ensues: by avoiding taking risks and experiencing both successes and failures, Puer types do not develop a sense of mastery. With their strengths and skills untested, they may have to grab onto their grandiose fantasies even more tightly, to try to maintain their sense of worth in the face of inevitable life challenges and the passing of time. Aging is probably their hardest and most tragic struggle, as sooner or later they run out of time to ever live out their grandiose narratives. As the author J. K. Rowling said in her commencement speech at Harvard University, "It is impossible to live without failing at something, unless you live so cautiously that you might as well not have lived at all—in which case, you fail by default."[8]

I have encountered many people who struggle to engage with their adult lives—people caught in Puer-type fantasies. When working with them in therapy, it has been of some value to explore how they came to be stuck in perpetual adolescence. Parents, of course, often played a role. Whether for an excess of caution or a desire to keep their children emotionally close, parents may have sheltered them from the unavoidable disappointments, discouraged commitment, and fed into fantasies of endless (future) possibilities. They may have overprotected and overprovided, without requiring effort and action. Parents who were too smothering may have made it hard for their children to give up the comforts provided to them; these young people may not see the advantages of establishing their own independent lives. Ultimately, however, I believe that the responsibility for one's life trajectory falls on each individual. Exploring our history, including how our parents affected us, is useful to understand ourselves, not to assign blame elsewhere. Puer types—as well as all of us, when tempted to retreat from adult responsibilities—must choose to give up unrealistic expectations and actively engage with their present lives.

I do not want to depict Puer types in an exclusively negative light, however. After all, they are correct in their observations that many people experience life as a dull, repetitive existence of duties and responsibilities, and that many sacrifice their youthful enthusiasm to the gods of propriety. On the contrary, people who hold onto their adolescent psychology tend to retain some of the excitement and freshness of those earlier years. And so Puer types, with their energy, freedom, and openness, remind us all that to be alive also means to be open to new beginnings and new possibilities.

Notes

1. Ovid, *Met*, IV.
2. For an overview, see von Franz, *Puer Aeternus*. Latin is a gendered language, and *puer* refers to male youth only, while *puella* would apply to girls. For simplicity and because gender differences may not be salient here, I use Puer for all genders.
3. von Franz, *Puer Aeternus*, 60.
4. Fitzgerald, *The Great Gatsby*, 98.
5. von Franz, *Puer Aeternus*.
6. de Saint-Exupéry, *The Little Prince*, 1–3.
7. von Franz, *Puer Aeternus*, 8.
8. Rowling, *Very Good Lives*, 34.

References

de Saint-Exupéry, A. *The Little Prince.* Translated by Katherine Woods. New York: Harcourt Brace & Company, 1943.
Fitzgerald, F. S. *The Great Gatsby.* New York: Scribner, 2004. First published 1925.
Rowling, J. K. *Very Good Lives: The Fringe Benefits of Failure and the Importance of Imagination.* New York: Little, Brown and Company, 2015.
von Franz, M.-L. *The Problem of the Puer Aeternus.* Toronto: Inner City Books, 2000.

5

SISYPHUS TYPE

Grandiosity in action

In contrast with Puer types, whose grandiose fantasies always remain unlived, there are people compelled by their grandiosity to relentlessly pursue extraordinary achievements. For them, the reveries are made into plans of attack, and the fantasies become concrete goals toward which they invest much effort, time, and resources. Not only they do not shy away from working hard for their dreams, but their grandiosity elicits a compulsive, all-encompassing dedication, which brings to mind the Sisyphean toil; hence, I call them Sisyphus types.[1]

The story of Sisyphus comes to us through Homer and Apollodorus, among others. In Greek mythology, Sisyphus was said to be the craftiest of all humans, clever to the point of being cunning. On numerous occasions, he tricked the gods themselves; for instance, when Thanatos—the personification of death—tried to bring him into the underworld, Sisyphus instead managed to chain death itself and save his own life (for a little while, at least). Interestingly, one of Sisyphus' ancestors was Prometheus, who as we know outwitted the gods too. Sisyphus and Prometheus, related by blood, seem to share the same grandiose gene.

Sisyphus is best known for his eternal task: pushing a huge stone up a hill, trying to bring it to the peak. And just as he is about to reach his goal, the stone tumbles back down to where he started. Each time, Sisyphus retraces his steps downhill and, "while the sweat pours from his limbs and the dust rises high above his head," he resumes lifting the stone, working his way toward the unattainable goal.[2]

Like the myth, Sisyphus types are completely devoted to their goals, which orient their whole lives. Often emerging in the shapeless fantasies of childhood, their goals at some point become set in stone; their early fantasies are taken literally. While Puer types are uncommitted and indecisive, Sisyphus types fully commit to their tasks, pushing away any doubt—other people's or their own. The toil becomes a necessity, as their sought-after goals are infused with many

32 Grandiose fantasies and strivings

"All the gold there is beneath the moon, and that there ever was, could not bring rest to any of these weary souls." Dante, *Inferno*. (Illustration by Gustave Doré, 1861.)

promises, including to gain an unbreakable sense of worth, specialness, and meaning—a permanent return to the original blissful state of infancy. And Sisyphus types truly believe that at some time in the future—due to their efforts, cleverness, or virtue—they will indeed accomplish their goals; they will finally reach the peak.

Sisyphus types may feel excited whenever there is progress—"This may be the time I finally get there. I see the finish line and cannot wait to cross it." However, since the compulsion never fully lifts, they more often feel stressed and anxious, if not empty. Periods of high energy and eagerness may alternate with feelings of exhaustion—a cycle that is triggered both by setbacks and the resurgence of their own unmet needs. Whenever they gain some insight into their struggles, they may experience their goals as a cage, an addiction, or a devilish something that possesses them.

So invested they are in their work, that they feel unable to stop and relax; downtime may quickly make them restless. More than simply driven, Sisyphus types seem single-minded and stubborn to other people, and are easily frustrated if distracted from their tasks. Their goals may determine everything they do, for example what books to read, social circles to join, foods to eat, hobbies to pursue, people to fall in love with, ways to spend their weekends, and topics worth discussing in conversations. Activities and people that are not instrumental in their quest may be considered unimportant, even a hindrance, and so they may be set aside.

The efforts required by such grandiose pursuits take a toll on both mind and body, and in many ways we could say that Sisyphus types age fast. I once worked with a young man, who had already determined in childhood that he did not want to "waste time" hanging out with friends, dating, playing sports, or learning about "useless topics," which for him included the humanities, fiction books, music, and anything that had to do with philosophical reflections on what makes life worth living. Compelled by grandiosity toward a profitable career, he invested all his energy in academic success. Additional summer courses, science camps, multiple majors, extra assignments, intensive tutoring—he was set on crushing it. To his classmates, he must have come across as someone who does not play or joke around, looking more like a serious adult than a peer. His parents, instead, were so proud that their child skipped adolescence and jumped right into the productive endeavors of adulthood. Surely, he was not having fun; he was also missing out on those experiences and idle time that may have helped him understand what made him happy and what else he might value in life beyond his career.

But Sisyphus types have no time to waste. Each week, day, even hour has to be productive and accounted for. Marissa Mayer, who was employee number 20 at Google and then went to become Yahoo's CEO, described in an interview her relationship with time.[3] She recounted that her success was due to her dedication and commitment, including working 130 hours each week—something that was apparently common among employees in the early years of Google. To work those many hours, Mayer said the trick was to be strategic about extraneous activities, like sleep and showers. She would do an all-nighter every week and rarely took a vacation. She even used to monitor the frequency of her bathroom breaks, lest they take too much time away from work. Biological needs are deemed unproductive hindrances—one wonders if Sisyphus had to wait for the stone to roll down so that he could take a bathroom break.

American values often align with Sisyphean strivings, with their emphasis on work, perseverance, and personal success. In the United States, when meeting somebody new—say, at a party—it is common for people to ask, "What do you do?" The idea is that a person's job speaks to who they are and what they are passionate about. It also provides an opportunity to break the ice and find out about shared interests to further the conversation. Italian culture, which generally leans toward the Puer type, does not focus on work as much. I have heard many Italians comment that asking about one's job at a social event is quite rude, similar to asking strangers about their yearly income. When asked about his job, an Italian friend of mine would reply, "You mean what I do … for fun? I cook, I read history books, I go for long walks…" In Italy, when meeting somebody for the first time, one usually focuses on relationships instead, for instance by asking, "Who do you know at this party? And how did you meet?"

In American schools, compulsive strivings are exalted, and perfectionism, a form of grandiosity, is highly valued. The grading system magnifies differences to incentivize effort. Percentiles, standardized scores, AP class requirements all suggest that knowledge and skills by themselves are not enough. One needs to do—and so *be*—better than everybody else. Similarly, American corporate culture prizes hard work and ambition, at times over collaboration, prudence, or ethical conduct. Employees' work lives center around the idea of skills advancement, increasing responsibilities, and promotions—the latter often based on employees' rankings. Hence, to be promoted, one has to outperform the competition, that is, one's own work friends. Seldom are people willing to say that they do not want to be considered for promotion, for instance because they may not be interested in taking on more responsibility or being required to do things they do not enjoy, like managing people. Climbing the career ladder reminds us of the Sisyphean hill; getting off of it often does not seem an option.

It is not just their employees; corporations themselves pursue grandiose strivings. In mission statements and in advertising, we can hear them affirm their goals to disrupt markets, radically innovate, transform people, change the world, and save the planet. At the same time, corporations declare that they will beat their competitors, grow to a monstrous size, and obtain huge financial returns. No corporation apparently can merely say, "I provide something useful and make some money by doing so."

If their grandiose compulsions center on work, Sisyphus types may do well financially. While spouses may complain that their partners spend too much time working and not enough with family, they too may revel in the upward mobility and financial rewards, reinforcing the compulsions as a desirable trait. Most often, there is an audience of spouses, parents, colleagues, and society at large that cheers on the grandiose efforts of the individual and—with their expectations—adds to the weight of the Sisyphean stone.

In some cases, Sisyphus types may be cunning and callous, under the philosophy that the end justifies the means. At a funding pitch, the founder of a start-up casually disclosed that he had invested in his venture all of his assets and some more: he had committed to it also his son's college funds. Yet, Sisyphus types may sincerely believe that their actions are noble, as they spring from their wish to be diligent, dutiful, and productive.

Investing effort, assets, and their reputation, Sisyphus types take their chances and so expose themselves to the risk of failure—while Puer types try to insure against it by living in a world of fantasy. Yet, Sisyphus types can also use fantasies, in their case to continuously reinterpret reality so that hard facts, setbacks, and negative feedback do not hinder their pursuits. Despite a history of bad investments and bankruptcies, Donald Trump said that he never failed at anything because— he thinks—he turned every loss into a big success.[4] The author J. K. Rowling employed a more sophisticated, but still grandiose, reinterpretation of reality when she found herself in a painful place in her life, long before gaining fame with her Harry Potter series. She was raising her daughter alone, poor, and jobless—and realized she had hit rock bottom. And yet, just at that moment, she was able to reconnect with her youthful desire to become a writer: "I was convinced that the only thing I wanted to do, ever, was to write novels."[5] She successfully managed to infuse her failures, no matter how painful, with meaning:

Failure meant a stripping away of the inessential. I stopped pretending to myself that I was anything other than what I was and began to direct all my energy into finishing the only work that mattered to me. Had I really succeeded at anything else, I might never have found the determination to succeed in the one arena where I believed I truly belonged. I was set free, because my greatest fear had been realized, and I was still alive, and I still had a daughter whom I adored, and I had an old typewriter and a big idea. And so rock bottom became the solid foundation on which I rebuilt my life.[6]

The fact remains that failures are sometimes unavoidable and unredeemable, regardless of our perseverance and the nobility of our aims. In Apulia, in southern Italy, a vase from ancient Greece recently resurfaced; it depicts Sisyphus pushing the stone while Ananke oversees his toil. Ananke is the goddess of fate and necessity, of the events that we cannot prevent or escape. Sigmund Freud considered her the personification of his "reality principle," those hard facts of life that we all, each in a different way, have to reckon with. Freud himself wrote that his decades-long battle with cancer was his struggle with Ananke.[7] And Sisyphus types may especially resent the constraints of reality and their own limitations, experiencing Ananke's presence as a frustrating burden.

Yet, it is the strength of Sisyphus types to persevere despite the challenges. From the outside, one cannot know whether their toil is or is not in vain. For most people, striving for extraordinary achievements proves futile, the stone destined to roll back to the foot of the hill. Some, however, may find a sense of meaning and purpose in their efforts, regardless of the costs paid along the way and of what was achieved in the end. And it may be possible that a few actually reach their sought-after goals, the heroic achievement of finally bringing the stone to rest at the peak.

Notes

1. The Jungian analyst Verena Kast offered a psychological exploration of the Sisyphus myth in *Sisyphus*.
2. Homer, *Odyssey*, 11.593–600. Translated by E.V. Rieu (London: Penguin Books, 1991).
3. Chafkin, "Yahoo's Marissa Mayer."
4. Barbaro, "What Drives Trump?"
5. Rowling, *Very Good Lives*, 15.
6. Rowling, *Very Good Lives*, 32–3.
7. See Schur, *Freud*, 357.

References

Barbaro, M. "What Drives Trump? A Fear of Fading Away." *New York Times*, October 25, 2016.
Chafkin, M. "Yahoo's Marissa Mayer on Selling a Company While Trying to Turn It Around." *Bloomberg Business Week*, August 4, 2016.

Kast, V. *Sisyphus: A Jungian Approach to Midlife Crisis.* Einsiedeln, Switzerland: Daimon Verlag, 1991.
Rowling, J. K. *Very Good Lives: The Fringe Benefits of Failure and the Importance of Imagination.* New York: Little, Brown and Company, 2015.
Schur, M. *Freud: Living and Dying.* New York: International Universities Press, 1972.

PART II
Everything can be hijacked by grandiosity

PART II

6

STORIES OF FAME, KNOWLEDGE, AND MONEY

> And still deeper the meaning of that story of Narcissus, who because he could not grasp the tormenting, mild image he saw in the fountain, plunged into it and was drowned. But that same image, we ourselves see in all rivers and oceans. It is the image of the ungraspable phantom of life; and this is the key to it all.
>
> Herman Melville, *Moby-Dick*

In 1968, an awesome sailing race—the Golden Globe race—was organized by the London *Sunday Times*. Starting in England, it required the circumnavigation of the whole earth, across the oceans, and around the dangerous Cape Horn. Participants had to sail solo, one person per boat, and without any stops along the way. This was a truly heroic undertaking, especially because it was before the time of GPS satellite tracking, reliable communications, and live weather forecasts. In case of an accident (and there were many), sailors would be left to their own devices in the middle of the sea. Being a grandiose undertaking, the race attracted the interest of a variety of sailors. Some had sailed across oceans already. Some were veterans of different record-breaking feats, including having rowed unassisted across the Atlantic Ocean. One was an ascetic sailor, Bernard Moitessier, who—after 304 days alone at sea—decided he did not care about the race after all and set sail for Tahiti.[1]

Among those who became interested in the race was Donald Crowhurst, an electrical engineer from a small town in England. Crowhurst was known among his friends for his imagination, intelligence, and gregariousness; he could talk for hours about his ideas and daring projects, many of which would only last the span of an evening. People described him as charismatic—a leading member of his town's amateur dramatist society—filled with contagious, youthful enthusiasm. On weekends, he sailed a small boat he owned, and in his free time he enjoyed reading biographies of famous sailors. He was a Puer type, creative and grandiose at the same time.

Throughout his life, he struggled to settle on a career. He was an airplane pilot for the Royal Air Force, but was dismissed for disciplinary reasons. He was an officer for the army, but crashed his car and tried to steal another—caught, he was dismissed again. Once he became an engineer, he went from job to job. An opinionated man, he seemed to grow restless whenever working for somebody else. He decided to start his own small company focusing on nautical equipment, Electron Utilisation. Soon, his company was struggling to stay in business. Crowhurst, always resourceful, convinced the wealthy businessman Stanley Best to invest in his company—an investment that did not pan out. Electron Utilisation was on the brink of bankruptcy when Crowhurst heard about the Golden Globe race and decided he wanted to participate.

That he was not prepared for such an undertaking may seem obvious, at least after the fact. And yet, at the time Crowhurst convinced his creditors, many expert sailors, a publicist, a boat maker, his wife, and his friends that he could indeed sail alone around the earth and win the race, bringing back honor and a considerable sum of money. Not only did they believe in him, but they also enabled and financed him. Stanley Best paid for a new custom-made boat—with the condition that, if Crowhurst did not finish the race, he would have to pay the money back. In an interview, Best said:

> I always considered Donald Crowhurst an absolutely brilliant innovator ... but as a businessman, as someone who had to know how the world went, he was hopeless. He was so much on the move all the time he never appreciated what was really happening. He seemed to have this capacity to convince himself that everything was going to be wonderful, and hopeless situations were only temporary setbacks. This enthusiasm, I admit, was infectious. But, as I now realize, it was the product of that kind of over-imaginative mind that was always dreaming reality into the state it wanted it to be.[2]

Crowhurst's own dreams were so powerful that he pushed away doubt and prudence. At one point, he penned out a chart where he "calculated" his average speed and those of his competitors, many of whom were expert sailors. His calculations "proved" that his innovative boat design, coupled with the untested futuristic technological devices he invented, would make him the fastest sailor. In *A Voyage for Madmen*, a book which chronicles the Golden Globe race, the author Peter Nichols, commented:

> The signal fault in his chart was his failure to allow for the wild card of the sea itself, the great leveler that always makes a mockery of men's best-laid plans, and the luck, good and bad, that is inevitably found there for one and all. Crowhurst's chart was the sort that could have been made only by a man who knew nothing of the sea.[3]

Because Crowhurst convinced himself, and everybody around him, that he would be able to complete and even win the race, he put himself in a bind. Anything short of first place would put his business and his family in dire straits. Caught by his dreams of glory, he committed to action his grandiose Puer fantasies—a jump from imagination to real life that proved fatal.

After many mishaps in the development and delivery of his boat and a rushed start off of England's coast, he struggled to advance on his competition as he sailed south in the Atlantic Ocean. As he wrote in his logbooks, Crowhurst came to the realization that his boat was unfit for the adventure and that he would not be able to win the race. Despite this, he journaled that he was unable and unwilling to sail back home to safety, given the shame and debt that would accompany defeat. Instead, he sailed for eight months aimlessly across the Atlantic. Via radio, he shared fake updates about his location and progress in the race, claiming exceptionally high speeds. He wondered if he could just say that he did circumnavigate the globe and then sail directly back to England to claim an undeserved victory. Being a Puer type but not a cheat, he found himself in an apparently impossible moral conflict and was overtaken by madness. His recovered logbooks detail his great confusion and mental agony; sadly, he is thought to have ultimately plunged into the ocean, dying by suicide—his sailboat found adrift a few days later by a passing ship.[4]

A different kind of sailor can be found in the story of Odysseus. Rumored to be the son of Sisyphus, he was similarly referred to as "Odysseus the Cunning" for his intelligence and craftiness. Greek mythology tells us that he was one of the kings who besieged Troy. After 10 years of war, he devised the trick of a wooden horse statue filled with soldiers to infiltrate the city and secure a final victory. As the various invading armies dismantled their siege camps, their kings and leaders returned to their respective homes. Odysseus, instead, embarked on a 10-year journey sailing around the known world. He survived encounters with a one-eyed Cyclops, cannibalistic tribes, hostile gods, and the tempting Sirens—creatures who lured sailors to shipwreck with their voices.

While he never forgot his native island Ithaca, where his wife Penelope and son Telemachus loyally awaited his return, he took the long way home and accrued knowledge and wisdom in the process. Ultimately, he returned home where he resumed his role as king and just ruler, as well as husband and father. Crowhurst and Odysseus were both driven by grandiose fantasies, whether hungry for fame, experiences, or knowledge. However, in the mythological account the latter was able, by strength of character or by destiny, to overcome his grandiosity and return home to his duties and rightful place in the order of life.

Reinterpreting the myth, the Italian poet Dante Alighieri imagined Odysseus restless and grandiose until the end. In his *La Divina Commedia*—in the first volume, titled *Inferno*, "Hell"—Dante wrote another ending for the Odysseus story. In Dante's version, Odysseus opted to shun his family and kingly responsibilities, deciding not to return to Ithaca. He was instead taken by a "burning desire" to pursue knowledge, "experience the world, and know the vices and virtues of

42 Everything can be hijacked by grandiosity

people."⁵ He embarked on a new adventure, this time sailing past the Strait of Gibraltar, between contemporary Spain and Morocco. The gods prohibited such a grandiose crossing, as the Mediterranean Sea was the known world, while the Strait led to unexplored seas. On Odysseus's desire for knowledge, Cicero wrote:

> So great is our innate love of learning and of knowledge, that no one can doubt that man's nature is strongly attracted to these things even without the lure of any profit. Do we notice how children cannot be deterred even by punishment from studying and inquiring into the world around them? Drive them away, and back they come. ... Again, take persons who delight in the liberal arts and studies; do we not see them careless of health or business, patiently enduring any inconvenience when under the spell of learning and of science ... It is knowledge that the Sirens offer, and it was no marvel if a lover of wisdom [Odysseus] held this dearer than his home.⁶

Dante's Odysseus convinced his crew to explore further, telling them, "You were not created to live as brutes, but to pursue virtue and knowledge."⁷ Out in the Ocean, they saw the mountaintop that humans were forbidden to reach: the Garden of Eden, the lost paradise from which humans were forever expelled. As soon as it became visible, Odysseus and his crew paid for their dare, and their explorations abruptly ended.

> Then a mountain appeared, dark
> in the distance, and it seemed so high,
> higher than I had ever seen before.
>
> We were elated, but the joy soon turned to tears;
> Because from this new land a tornado was born
> That struck the prow of our boat.
>
> Three times it made us spin with all the waters,
> On the fourth it lifted the stern,
> And pushed the bow down, as it pleased the Other,
>
> Until the ocean closed in over us again.⁸

Odysseus, his crew, and his ship were swallowed by the deep open sea, their lives claimed yet again by the Atlantic Ocean. Dante depicted Odysseus with great respect and admiration; after all, Dante too was an explorer, as in his poetry he imagined visiting the afterlife itself. But ultimately in *La Divina Commedia*, Dante placed Odysseus in Hell because of the excesses of his desire for knowledge. As a cautionary tale, Odysseus's fate seems to suggest that unrestrained grandiosity is ultimately defeated; a destiny that Crowhurst experienced firsthand.

Another kind of exploration was the one undertaken by Carl Jung, a Sisyphus type. In addition to his training as a physician and psychiatrist, he extensively studied world mythology, foreign languages, alchemy, religious treatises, and literature. He wrote and illustrated a 200-page manuscript to record his dreams and

Stories of fame, knowledge, and money **43**

fantasies, recently published under the title *The Red Book*.⁹ His encyclopedic knowledge and deep thinking on these varied subjects were poured into more than 20 tomes of writing. He too was driven by an "insatiable drive toward understanding," in his case seeking knowledge of the symbols and manifestations of the unconscious.¹⁰ "The daimon of creativity has ruthlessly had its way with me," he wrote in his autobiography *Memories, Dreams, Reflections*. "The ordinary undertakings I planned usually had the worst of it—though not always and not everywhere."¹¹

The costs of one's grandiosity are often borne by spouses and children. Dante's Odysseus never returned to his family. Crowhurst left his wife in a dire financial situation and his children without a father. Jung spent his days and nights researching and writing about psychology. Reflecting back on his relationships, toward the end of his life Jung wrote:

> I have offended many people, for as soon as I saw that they did not understand me, that was the end of the matter so far as I was concerned. I had to move on. I had no patience with people—aside from my patients. I had to obey an inner law which was imposed on me and left me no freedom of choice. … For some people I was continually present and close to them so long as they were related to my inner world; but then it might happen that I was no longer with them, because there was nothing left which would link me to them. I had to learn painfully that people continued to exist even when they had nothing more to say to me. Many excited in me a feeling of living humanity, but only when they appeared within the magic circle of psychology; next moment, when the spotlight cast its beam elsewhere, there was nothing to be seen.¹²

Human desires are often more prosaic than the pursuit of knowledge. Fabulous Fab—as Fabrice Tourre was nicknamed by his friends—was an ambitious 20-something trader for a large bank. He contributed to the creation and sale of "synthetic collateralized debt obligations"—the complex and volatile financial instruments at the center of the 2008 financial crisis. As the markets started to show signs of weakness, Tourre wrote to his then-girlfriend:

> More and more leverage in the system. The whole building is about to collapse anytime now…Only potential survivor, the fabulous Fab…standing in the middle of all these complex, highly leveraged, exotic trades he created without necessarily understanding all of the implications of those monstruosities!!!¹³

A few days later, he added:

> When I think that I had some input into the creation of this product (which by the way is a product of pure intellectual masturbation, the type of thing

which you invent telling yourself: "Well, what if we created a "thing", which has no purpose, which is absolutely conceptual and highly theoretical and which nobody knows how to price?") it sickens the heart to see it shot down in mid-flight... It's a little like Frankenstein turning against his own inventor;)[14]

Tourre's reference to Frankenstein, the archetypal monster of recent times, is apt. Mary Shelley's original story—*Frankenstein or the Modern Prometheus*—narrated the life and fall of Victor Frankenstein, a scientist who created a living creature from corpses, yet another grandiose fantasy that yields monstrosities.

Hopefully, with enough awareness, we can catch glimpses of the financial monstrosities we create: we may buy houses we cannot afford because banks are willing to lend us the money; we may never look at our bank statements and remain unaware of our spending or debt; we may pursue risky investments that we do not understand, eager to make high returns; we may wrongly believe we have unique insights about a stock or a financial opportunity, exposing ourselves to unwarranted risks as we pursue profit. Each of these is an expression of grandiose fantasies, a monstrosity that we convince ourselves we can safely sail to shore. With statistical regularity, lured by promises of success and wealth, we end up being swallowed by these Sirens of our modern times.

Tourre was found liable for defrauding investors. After making millions of dollars during his tenure at the bank, he paid less than one million back. He did not admit guilt and instead decided to simply move on to the next chapter of his life: academic research. The University of Chicago welcomed him into their doctorate of economics, where—ironically—he worked in the field of bank regulation. His doctoral advisor considered him one of his most promising students. Clearly, a good outcome for him, although arguably less so from an accountability perspective.

The current iteration of grandiose fantasies of wealth is the goal of creating the next big start-up. Start-ups have the lure of being accessible to all, even to those with little initial capital. Supposedly, all it takes is having an idea that "disrupts the market" and scaling it to enormous size: millions of dollars will follow. And by focusing on the success stories alone, this narrative is continuously reinforced. Some people may become addicted to the energy and intensity of starting new business ventures and turn into serial entrepreneurs.

In 1977, a Stanford MBA named Roy Raymond opened a lingerie store in Palo Alto, California. Designed to appeal to men buying gifts for their partners, it had a distinctive décor compared to traditional department stores; Raymond called it Victoria's Secret. After a few years, owning what had become a small chain of five stores plus a mail-order catalog, Raymond sold it for an amount now equivalent to two-and-a-half million dollars—it was the new owner that transformed the brand into a worldwide phenomenon. After he sold, Raymond decided to pursue a new idea, investing all his money to open My Child's Destiny, a store offering high-end children's products. However, this venture did not fare well. Raymond went bankrupt, and his family—a wife and their two children—lost houses and savings. After My Child's Destiny, Raymond opened a children's bookstore, which also failed. He then borrowed money from his mother and started another company, a home repair hardware business, which fared the same. After a decade spent trying to start new ventures, 47-year-old Raymond jumped off the Golden Gate Bridge.[15] Notably, Raymond's cautionary tale is currently taught at MBA programs, but only to argue against selling too soon, lest losing *potential* future money. On the contrary, it seems to me that this tale points to the importance of slowing down a little: slowing down our imagination, as well as our actions.

While some make the toil for money their only focus, it would be a mistake to always associate money with grandiosity. After all, we all need to work and make a living. It is Puer types who claim that earning an income is not important and that money will come (from somewhere, from someone), freeing them to focus on so-called higher endeavors in the spiritual, artistic, and social realms. And so, money always remains an ambiguous entity, caught in between the extremes of infinite wealth and renunciation.

"But how much money is enough money?" I asked my friend, a banker who had made many sacrifices in his life to advance his career. He answered, "When I have enough money that I don't have to worry about it anymore." The reality is that we do not know what our lives have in store for us; we cannot save for and insure against all risks. Hence, we cannot ever eliminate the "problem of money," so to say, making this project a grandiose one. The fact that worries about money happen at any wealth level bears testament to this impossibility.

Notes

1. Bernard Moitessier's own account of the race and his decision to quit it and pursue other goals is a classic book in sailing literature and beyond: *The Long Way*.
2. Tomalin and Hall, *Strange Voyage*, 20.
3. Nichols, *A Voyage for Madmen*, 80.
4. Crowhurst's story, including excerpts from his logbooks, is narrated by Tomalin and Hall, *Strange Voyage*.
5. Dante, *Inferno*, XXVI, 98–99. My translation.
6. Cicero, *De Finibus*, 5.18. Translated by H. Rackham. New York: Macmillan, 1914.
7. Dante, *Inferno*, XXVI, 119–120.
8. Dante, *Inferno*, XXVI, 133–142.
9. Jung, *Red Book*.
10. Jung, *Memories, Dreams, Reflections*, 322.
11. Jung, *Memories, Dreams, Reflections*, 358.
12. Jung, *Memories, Dreams, Reflections*, 357.
13. Securities and Exchange Commission v. Goldman, Sachs & Co. and Fabrice Tourre, 10 Civ. 3229 (BJ).
14. U.S. Senate, Committee on Homeland Security and Governmental Affairs, Permanent Subcommittee on Investigations, Hearing on Wall Street and the Financial Crisis: The Role of Credit Rating Agencies, Additional Exhibits, 2010.
15. "Roy Raymond," *New York Times*, September 02, 1993.

References

Jung, C. G. *Memories, Dreams, Reflections*. New York: Vintage Books, 1989.
Jung, C. G. *The Red Book: A Reader's Edition*. New York: Norton & Company, 2009.
Moitessier, B. *The Long Way*. Dobbs Ferry, NY: Sheridan House, 1995. First published 1971.
Nichols, P. *A Voyage for Madmen*. New York: HarperCollins, 2001.
"Roy Raymond, 47; Began Victoria's Secret," *New York Times*, September 02, 1993.
Tomalin, N. and R. Hall. *The Strange Voyage of Donald Crowhurst*. Camden, Maine: International Marine/McGraw-Hill, 1995.

7

STORIES OF BEAUTY, YOUTH, PERFECTION—AND NARCISSISM

> Five hours, (and who can do it less in?)
> By haughty Celia spent in dressing;
> The goddess from her chamber issues,
> Arrayed in lace, brocades and tissues. ...
> Strephon, who found the room was void, ...
> Stole in, and took a strict survey, ...
> So Strephon lifting up the lid,
> To view what in the chest was hid.
> The vapors flew from out the vent, ...
> Disgusted Strephon stole away
> Repeating in his amorous fits,
> Oh! Celia, Celia, Celia shits!
>
> Jonathan Swift, *The Lady's Dressing Room*

"Once upon a time in the middle of winter, when snowflakes the size of feathers were falling from the sky, a queen was sitting and sewing"—so begins the "Snow White" fairy tale.[1] It was recorded in 1812 by Jacob and Wilhelm Grimm—the brothers Grimm—as they collected folk and fairy tales in Germany's countryside. These were stories shared around the fire and in spinning circles, transmitted orally from one generation to the next. Even if the Grimms titled their collection *Nursery and Household Tales*, their book was initially intended for a scholarly audience, for adults; after all, it contained gory violence and explicit—often incestuous—sex. By their time, these tales were considered "lesser" literature, a vestige of folk traditions that the Grimms wanted to save and honor. "The custom of telling tales ... is on the wane," they wrote, "just as all the cozy corners in homes and in gardens are giving way to an empty splendor that resembles the smile with which one speaks of these tales."[2] Telling tales, they added, was a custom that persisted "in places where there is a warm openness to poetry or where there are imaginations not yet deformed by the perversities of modern life."[3]

Imagination is indeed needed to allow fairy tales to resonate with our modern sensibilities. And when interpreted psychologically, these tales become opportunities to learn about ourselves. Many interpretative approaches have been proposed, but I focus on the Jungian approach in particular.[4] Because fairy tales clearly separate the good characters—who are often also naive—from the villains who oppose them, we may be tempted (yet again) to identify with the positive heroes and to despise the evil ones. After all, on the surface, many stories present a clear moral lesson, with the heroes prevailing while the villains are punished for their excesses—beware! However, a Jungian approach to fairy tales—as well as to mythological stories and even our personal nighttime dreams—invites us to consider all the characters in a story as representations of different parts of our own psychology as they interact and collide with each other. Fairy tales then are seen as depicting our vulnerable and naive sides together with the demanding and unreasonable ones, whose critical voices we often carry within. Interpreted this way, fairy tales can offer templates for personal transformation and opportunities for self-knowledge.[5]

Among the many tales, the story of Snow White has become popular and widely interpreted.[6] In our exploration of the various forms of grandiosity, Snow White highlights fantasies centered on the body, such as fantasies about youth, beauty, and perfection. Looking at snow-covered fields outside her window—the story goes—the queen wished for a child. When her wish came true, she called her daughter Snow White. In the more widely circulated version of the tale, the queen suddenly died, leaving her daughter in the care of an evil stepmother. Interestingly, this was not the case in the first edition of *Nursery and Household Tales*: it was Snow White's mother who happened to be the evil queen.[7]

Having a child was not the queen's only wish, as she also wished for (her own) extraordinary beauty. "Mirror, mirror, on the wall, who's the fairest one of all?"[8] For a while, the mirror reassuringly confirmed that she was the most beautiful of all, and her self-esteem was preserved. Things changed, however, when Snow White grew up. When asked again, the mirror changed its tune: "My queen, you may be the fairest here, but Snow White is a thousand times more fair."[9] The queen was consumed by this realization, her grandiosity challenged because "unless she herself was the fairest in the land, she would never be able to feel anything but envy."[10] As a result, she ordered a hunter to bring her Snow White's lungs and liver, planning to eat them. When the hunter failed to kill the queen's daughter, she resolved to take things into her own hands and repeatedly poisoned Snow White, including with the famous apple. Thinking her daughter dead, her "envious heart was finally at peace, as much as an envious heart can be."[11] We know that in the end Snow White prevails, but in the meantime what a remarkable display of envy and rage.

We are left wondering what it is the queen saw in the mirror that would trigger such rage. After all, when we stand alone in front of a mirror, what we see and hear are our own thoughts and preoccupations about ourselves. Being so focused on her appearances—and caught in impossible comparisons—the queen might have seen the passing of time and the inevitable changes brought upon by aging. Sadly, she was aghast by them.

Grandiose ideals of perfection and eternal youth can affect us all, just as they do the characters of fairy tales. Cosmetics advertising cunningly titillates our fantasies: we buy anti-aging lotions and firming moisturizers—modern-day potions that promise to slow down the passage of time or even revert it. Because demand creates its own supply, the medical field has been investing millions in cosmetics scientific research. Botulinum Toxin is a neurotoxin that causes paralysis; throughout history, it has killed humans whenever ingested through contaminated food—something akin to poisoned apples. Nowadays it is also marketed as Botox, because it was discovered that when injected locally in small doses, it paralyzes only our facial muscles, temporarily reducing the depth of our wrinkles. Millions of people seek Botox every year, trading the expressiveness of their facial features for a younger, more ethereal appearance. Even the websites of medical professional organizations shamelessly suggest we create "wish lists" of cosmetic surgeries. Among the options, the "mommy makeover" promises to undo the effects of childbirth on women's bodies.

Surely, fantasies of beauty and youthfulness affect all genders. While the adolescent boy often awaits with trepidation the first appearance of facial hair, many men soon despise the physical manifestations of their aging, such as their white hair and the receding hairlines they so carefully monitor at the mirror. Even clothing styles are chosen to project a younger image—this is the domain of the Puer, pushing us to hold onto our youth. And indeed, aging is a scary thing, as our bodies weaken and slow down, and pains and chronic illnesses become more common. However, our resistance to this inevitable process makes the experience harder than it needs to be. For instance, hearing loss is often left unaddressed, not for lack of remedies, but for the self-image implications of wearing hearing aids.

I do not want to downplay how other people's responses to our appearances can influence our sense of identity and self-esteem. However, if we put too much weight on external validation, we risk feeding our insecurities, never quite settling into our bodies and lives. The emergence of the Internet has amplified the focus on appearances like never before. As any bus ride or airport lounge shows, we are all mesmerized looking at the screens of our phones—the distorted mirrors of our time. They are distorted because through them we are bombarded with images of beauty, youth, and strength that are so manipulated and falsified that reality and fantasy blur together. While in the past there were only so many attractive and compelling folks in our schools and neighborhoods, nowadays multitudes of them are showed on TV, advertisements, and online.

Social media amplifies this fiction and allows us to join in the production of perfectly curated, filtered, angled pictures of ourselves—the "five minutes of celebrity" have become the "fifty likes of popularity." Ultimately, we are continually stimulated by the possibility of being seen and of being responded to—our sense of worth dependent on the response of our "followers." The risk is that we end up venerating images with no soul, taking as alive what are only flat illusions.

◆

The problem of pursuing illusions is an old one, older than social media. In Jonathan Swift's 1732 poem quoted at the beginning of this chapter, suitor Strephon had too partial a view of his beloved lady, Celia. By invasively surveying her dressing room, he discovered the obvious: Celia was beautiful—her name means "heavenly"—but still human, a fact that shocked him. In relationships, the realities of the body shatter grandiose fantasies of perennial enchantment. In my work with couples, I heard more than a few arguments about farting: on whether it was human, too human, or pure abomination.[12]

Grandiosity about the body may also show in boundary-testing and death-defying endeavors. Recently, several men have fallen off skyscrapers, as it has become popular to climb to the top of buildings without protection to take "selfies." An audience is always present, as the climb is broadcasted, streaming live on social media. Extreme sports share a similar mindset, that is to challenge the reality of gravity and all the other laws of nature, as people dive from cliffs, climb without safety harnesses, walk on ropes, jump from airplanes to fly with "wingsuits," and roll off mountains on all kinds of wheeled things. Many practitioners of these sports describe these experiences as "freeing"; it is indeed the (temporary) lifting of the limitations of the body that feels freeing, together with the denial of our mortality.

The quest for productivity and efficiency—another grandiose endeavor—hijacks the relationship with our bodies too. I remember my grandfather falling asleep after lunch, sitting up on the couch. This was Italy, and this was many decades ago. It was a 30-minute nap, and he would return to his office refreshed and unrushed. Having the luxury of a couch in my office, I try to keep this family tradition alive. But nowadays naps are out of fashion: we are told that they are a symptom of laziness. Unless, that is, we present scientific evidence on how they restore brain functioning and increase productivity at work; unless we reframe them as "power naps."

On our quest for productivity, we push our bodies into activity and frenzy. For instance, I have worked with several students who had panic attacks and were unable to think clearly, all because they had forgotten to sleep—even two nights in a row—to study for final exams. For others, it was too many cups of coffee that triggered unbearable anxiety, if not the stimulants bought from their friends and used without prescription. And I know of a married couple who would take stimulants—the same amphetamines they used to party when they were younger—to clean and tidy up their home; they felt that without stimulants they would waste time being unproductive. At night, they put themselves to sleep with cannabis, because they struggled to stop thinking about their to-do lists and work.

The underlying fantasy is that we should never feel bored, sad, or tired; these are seen as problems we should treat away, obstacles to our search for perfect happiness. For this ideal, we abuse alcohol, opioids, stimulants, marijuana, and many other substances, as we seek the perfect mix of relaxation and euphoria, focused attention and relief from negative emotions—all on our schedule and available on demand. With these magic potions, the ego seeks to reign supreme on our emotions and biological needs. Relating to our bodies as something to control, we become unable to distinguish if we are tired, excited, vulnerable, sleepy, hungry, or comfortable—so we do not know what we need in any given moment. Caught by fantasies of how our bodies "should" feel, we find ourselves estranged from the intuitive wisdom emerging from our physical sensations.

Among all inborn and biological drives, sexuality plays a central role in our lives and especially in our fantasies, so much that the word "fantasy" is often used to refer to sexual fantasies. Sexuality is made of wishes of uncertain fulfillment, dependent on whether other people reciprocate our interest, and also on our—often puzzling and unconscious—desires. Because of these uncertainties, sexuality can evoke anxieties related to sharing, rejection, and vulnerability.

To try to avoid these anxieties, our grandiosity can hijack sexuality, bringing forth yet another fantasy of control. For instance, the first sexual encounters, which can be as meaningful as they are overwhelming, are nowadays spoiled by Viagra and pornography. I worked with a young man in his early twenties who had never had sex—and who did not have a partner either—but who always carried (physician prescribed) Viagra in his backpack, just in case. He did not want to risk losing an erection if the opportunity for sex were to arise—interpreting the core of the "first time" experience as a matter of performance. Similarly, pornography eliminates any specialness from the "unveiling" and our first encounters, limiting our freedom to discover over time our own, personal approach to sexual intimacy.

Grandiosity can also transform sexuality into a frantic search for always new and ever exciting sexual encounters, whether they be actual or just fantasy. On weekends, a wealthy man would take escorts on vacation to exotic resorts, binging on sex and cocaine. He was disappointed to discover again and again that after such artificially expansive (and expensive) experiences—a crazy weekend, the wild encounters—that he always had to return back to the realities of his life, including his usual depressed mood. When we compulsively seek emotionally and physically charged experiences, we look for a high that will not last. When the inebriation—due to attraction, drugs, or physical stimulation—is gone, then what?

Grandiose fantasies of perfection and youth can also hijack parenthood. For instance, some new parents may pursue the impossible fantasy of a do-over of their own childhood: by caring for their children, they hope to undo their own old wounds. Children can be recruited as insurance against boredom, loneliness, and the dread of old age—all the way to fantasies of leaving a legacy and immortality. Unsure about their purpose in life, some may overidentify with their role as parents and cling to the intensity of the parent-child connection—the "high" of feeling needed and loved—only to grow resentful when their children establish new relationships and embrace different perspectives.

To be thin, full-haired, voluptuous, wrinkle-free, muscular, productive, young, indestructible, potent, immortal, needed… this is the grandiose project: to mold ourselves into an ideal form, into something that we are not (at least not anymore, not all the time). And so, this is a project destined to fail when confronted by the passage of time and inevitable changes in our lives.

"And still deeper the meaning of that story of Narcissus…" begins the quote by Herman Melville that opened the previous chapter. The story of Narcissus, as narrated by the Roman poet Ovid in his *Metamorphoses*, opens with Narcissus as a child, "a child with whom one could have fallen in love even in his cradle."[13] And as a young man, he continued to attract the interest of many men and women alike. But he loved none of them back, all the while scorning and mocking these suitors with a "pride so unyielding."[14] When a nymph made a bolder attempt to approach him, Narcissus uttered aloud, "Away with these embraces! I would die before I would have you touch me!"[15] The story tells us that when the gods heard that Narcissus was mistreating all of his suitors, they decided to punish him by making him fall in love with an unattainable "person"—the man who did not love anyone, was now to fall in love with his own image. One day, Narcissus arrived at a spring to drink and he laid down near the pool of shining silvery waters.

> While he sought to quench his thirst, another thirst grew in him, and as he drank, he was enchanted by the beautiful reflection that he saw. He fell in love with an insubstantial hope, mistaking a mere shadow for a real body. Spellbound by his own self, he remained there motionless, with fixed gaze, like a statue … Unwittingly, he desired himself, and was himself the object of his own approval, at once seeking and sought, himself kindling the flame with which he burned. How often did he vainly kiss the treacherous pool, how often plunge his arms deep in the waters, as he tried to clasp the neck he saw! But he could not lay hold upon himself. He did not know what he was looking at, but was fired by the sight, and excited by the very illusion that deceived his eyes.[16]

Whenever Narcissus looked away from the water, his reflection—and so his loved one—would disappear, causing him sorrow. So, he remained at the pool, distraught. "What I desire, I have. My very plenty makes me poor," he exclaimed.[17] Ultimately, he pined away—he withered because of grief and longing—and died. In other, earlier versions of the myth, however, Narcissus actually killed himself

"What I desire, I have. My abundance has made me poor." Ovid, *Metamorphoses*. (Illustration by Étienne Delaune, Narcissus, 1569.)

once he realized the impossibility of his desire.[18] And we wonder, then, what it is that Narcissus desired, but no one can have.

The term narcissism, of course, derives from the story of Narcissus and his obsession with himself. Initially, the term was proposed by Havelock Ellis and then separately by Paul Näcke to describe those who love (supposedly, too much) their own bodies, that is, those who look at, masturbate, and find pleasure in themselves. The term was later adopted by Freud in a seminal paper published in 1914, *On Narcissism: An Introduction*. Rather than focusing on the idea of vanity or the excesses of masturbation, Freud began exploring how narcissism may describe specific ways of relating to ourselves and other people in our lives. However, Freud did not elaborate on his ideas past his *Introduction*, and narcissism did not play a central role in his theories. Yet, based on Freud's one paper alone, the concept of narcissism—the idea that we may invest considerable energy in "loving" ourselves—has continued to intrigue psychologists over the last 100 years. Many have interpreted Freud's original thoughts and expanded upon them.

Among the many definitions and reinterpretations, narcissism has been associated with the original blissful state of childhood ("primary narcissism") and with the healthy childhood grandiosity that leads to the establishment of self-esteem, both of which were discussed in chapter 2.[19] Narcissism has also been associated with a problematic and dominating way of relating to people, which is what we explore here.

The psychoanalyst Otto Kernberg, informed by his work with narcissistic patients, painted a troublesome description of their psychology—troublesome even when these patients are successful professionally and socially:

> These patients present an unusual degree of self-reference in their interactions with other people, a great need to be loved and admired by others, and a curious apparent contradiction between a very inflated concept of themselves and an inordinate need for tribute from others. Their emotional life is shallow. They experience little empathy for the feelings of others, they obtain very little enjoyment from life other than from the tributes they receive from others or from their own grandiose fantasies, and they feel restless and bored when external glitter wears off and no new sources feed their self-regard. They envy others, tend to idealize some people from whom they expect narcissistic supplies and to depreciate and treat with contempt those from whom they do not expect anything (often their former idols). In general, their relationships with other people are clearly exploitative and sometimes parasitic. It is as if they feel they have the right to control and possess others and to exploit them without guilt feelings—and, behind a surface which very often is charming and engaging, one senses coldness and ruthlessness.[20]

The self-reference, the need to be admired, the ruthlessness—these traits remind us of the original myth of Narcissus. In the version of the myth told by Ovid, unique among Narcissus' suitors was the nymph Echo. What was peculiar about her was that she could only repeat other people's words, she could not speak with her own—hence her name. Having fallen in love with Narcissus, she resolved to follow him around the woods. Ovid so described their courtship:

> The boy, by chance, had wandered away from his faithful band of comrades, and he called out: "Is there anybody here?" Echo answered: "Here!" Narcissus stood still in astonishment, looking round in every direction, and cried at the pitch of his voice: "Come!" As he called, she called in reply. He looked behind him, and when no one appeared, cried again: "Why are you avoiding me?" But all he heard were his own words echoed back. Still he persisted, deceived by what he took to be another's voice, and said, "Come here, and let us meet!" Echo answered: "Let us meet!" ... she came out of the wood and made to throw her arms round the neck she loved.[21]

In spite of his initial flirting with Echo, things became "too real" for Narcissus. Had he engaged, then a relationship could have developed and mutual feelings emerged. But Narcissus could not risk feeling vulnerable. That was when he cried, "Away with these embraces! I would die before I would have you touch me!"[22] Thus scorned, Echo "concealed herself in the woods … in lonely caves … and, though never seen, … is heard by all."[23] It seems relevant that Narcissus would be in a relationship, as brief as it was, with Echo, with somebody who could only present back to Narcissus his own words.

My experiences working with narcissistic patients come to mind. Over the years, I have indeed encountered people who became upset, irritated, or at times even angry whenever I would share some of my thoughts during our conversations. For instance, my contribution may have been a different approach to a problem they described. Other times, when my patients were struggling in their relationships with spouses, friends, or parents, I may have suggested they try to imagine the other person's needs and point of view. Sometimes, I resorted to simply offer a summary of what I thought they had just shared—but even these interjections were met with hostility, as I was told that my choice of words was off. It truly felt that I could only echo their words back to them, or alternatively I should stay silent session after session. Any real exchange and communication would break down.[24]

I have since come to understand that my comments were perceived as unwelcome appearances of otherness and difference. And it is the hate of difference that is the core of narcissism.[25] To some degree, we all dislike differences. Instinctually, we may interpret whatever breaks a pattern as dangerous; for instance, when we catch a glimpse of something moving within the stillness of the background, like a snake in the vegetation. We may resent what breaks our routines and forces its way into our mind, homes, and lives. We may struggle to warm up to and trust new people, all the more when they do not look like us or come from the same cultural backgrounds. We tend to resist new ideas and perspectives, while our comfort zone is often limited to those social circles that validate our own worldviews and values. Like our immune system, which detects and reacts to what does not belong within our bodies, we too detect and respond to differences, to what we perceive as "other" than us.

The Jungian analyst Marcus West proposed that our preference for sameness and distaste toward difference fundamentally shape our lives. While it may seem that people are motivated by the pursuit of pleasure, happiness, meaning, or power, West suggested that we most fundamentally seek what is familiar to us.[26] The word "familiar" immediately links us back to our past and to our parents. And indeed, we often engage with people and situations through the lenses shaped by our early life experiences and the role models we witnessed, above all, our parents. Beyond our personal histories, "familiar" also refers to anything consistent with our worldviews, our sense of identity, and our established sources of self-esteem. In other words, it is the ego that seeks what is familiar, and what is familiar to the ego is itself—who we think we are, and especially who we *like* to think of ourselves as.

The unfamiliar and other, however, inevitably enters our lives, from the outside and from within ourselves. From the outside—through new situations and people we encounter—we are confronted by ideas, needs, and emotions that are surely a source of difference, never being completely attuned to our needs or compliant with our wishes. Our own thoughts and feelings can challenge our desire for sameness too, whenever they defy the way we would rather feel in a given moment. For example, we may be caught by surprise when we realize that we are feeling insecure at a social gathering. Or we may be disappointed when we suddenly realize that we have been feeling depressed for a while. Even the realization that we are falling in love can be anxiety provoking, as it represents a challenge to our preference for control. Seeking sameness, we can narcissistically perceive any challenging situation, encounter, or inner experience as other, foreign, and ultimately unwanted.[27]

West wrote that this "basic narcissistic mechanism" operates within all of us. From time to time, we all can exhibit some measure of narcissism, especially whenever we feel emotionally vulnerable or physically tired. At those times, we retreat into our comfort zone and become less open to difference and newness.[28] Some people, however, tend to get stuck in the narcissistic mode. Rather than opening up to the inevitable frustrations that accompany relationships, they may try to dominate interactions and other people, seeking only loyal admirers and constant validation. Rather than accepting the often-contradictory feelings, thoughts, and fantasies that spring up from the unconscious, they solely identify with their narrowest egos—a desire to be fully in control of their inner lives, to the point of denying even having an inner life. Any step outside of their comfort zone is accompanied by strong emotions—anxieties, fears, rage—just as those patients of mine reacted with frustration and anger to my interjections.

In the myth, what Narcissus wished for but could not get was the disappearance of otherness. Enamored with his own reflection, the ego loved itself and nothing more. But this love is too narrow, and it saps all vitality, causing Narcissus's life to end.[29] So radical is the wish of narcissism—to eliminate otherness, vulnerability, and dependency—that it is always grandiose, an impossible fantasy of denying the realities of our inner lives and of our relationships.

But the reverse is not true: grandiosity does not always imply narcissism. For instance, one could think of monks or ascetics who choose to live in isolation, spending time praying and meditating in a remote monastery or, as they used to, in a mountain cave; their goals may be self-knowledge, devotion, or getting closer to the gods. Or one could consider the lives of the explorers and sailors who challenge themselves with incredible adventures, like the stories I presented in the previous chapter. Their isolation, surely, creates a situation where they cannot escape from themselves, having removed the ways we usually numb and distract ourselves from our thoughts and feelings. All these people—and many others—may pursue grandiose goals without trying to dominate other people or suppress their own inner experiences. It is important to reclaim our freedom to be grandiose, provided that we are being true to ourselves and do not use others as a means to an end.

I once worked with a couple who was full of resentment. He was an accountant at a large firm, and he squarely fit the stereotype of accountants. He was dedicated to his work, conscientious, and parsimonious with money while also being financially successful, a Sisyphus type who was—to use his word—boring. She instead was full of creative ideas, playful, extroverted, hopelessly stuck in a doctorate, not concerned with ever finding a job, and overwhelmed by her many interests and passions—a Puer type, who had grand fantasies about avenues to express her creativity but little discipline to bring any to fruition. This could have been a perfect match: each driving the other crazy with their differences, but also creating an opportunity for joining forces and building on their complementary strengths. However, this favorable outcome would have required self-awareness and open negotiation. He could have financed their lives (without underlying resentment), and in exchange she could have brought a measure of vitality that he so sorely needed. Why, otherwise, would they have found each other and fallen in love in the first place? Their grandiose fantasies—of success for him, of explorations for her—could have been accommodated in their relationship. Instead, they tried to control one another, to persuade the other that their own approach to life was best, and to morph the other into themselves—an approach that killed the possibility of real connection and mutual transformation.

The reasons why some relate narcissistically to their inner lives and to other people have been widely debated among psychoanalytic authors. There is no doubt that early life experiences, as shaped by one's own parents, leave a lasting impression. If a person had depressed, unpredictable, hostile, or uninterested parents, then fundamental questions—questions such as whether people are reliable and caring, or whether one's own feelings and thoughts are safe to accept—could be answered in the negative, and for good reason. Some authors argued that these types of early experiences cause narcissism.[30] The Jungian analyst Neville Symington offered a different perspective. He also understood narcissism as a defense against vulnerability, usually erected early in life as a result of trauma or an emotionally arid family life. However, Symington maintained that narcissism is always a choice, though an unconscious one.[31] "Unconscious choice" is an interesting term, as it embraces the possibility of change—if it is a choice, we can choose otherwise—while also illuminating how unaware we might be of our narcissistic frame of mind, that we may be repressing otherness wherever it presents itself. In the myth, Narcissus seems to think that because he loves his reflection so much, then he can never leave the pool where he saw it, and pines away. One wonders if he was actually free to let go of his mirrored image, his grandiose fantasies of beauty, perfection, and sameness. Leaving the spring, he could have opened up to otherness and difference, embracing the trepidation brought on by a new, unfamiliar choice.

◆

What we see in our mirrors can be deceiving, as the stories of Snow White and Narcissus show, because we may obsess on the narrowest idea of who we are and of what is valuable and beautiful in us. However, mirrors are not only symbols of vanity and self-absorption, but also of self-knowledge. We may wonder, then, where we can find better mirrors, mirrors that help us learn about ourselves in more useful and objective ways.

"The precursor of the mirror is the mother's face," wrote Donald Winnicott.[32] Wondering what infants see when they look around, Winnicott argued that the first thing they see is the face of their mothers. And mothers attuned to the experiences of their children—as most mothers are—are looking back at them, responding to their smiles and cries, to their emotional states, and to their play. It is in the interactions with their mothers, Winnicott argued, that children begin to see and know themselves.[33] I would add that in the interactions with their parents, children also encounter otherness for the first time, for instance, whenever there are misunderstandings and competing needs between children and their parents.

We find mirrors for self-knowledge not only in the empathic gaze of our parents, but also in the faces of all those we interact with in our lives. If we approach these encounters with vulnerability and openness to feedback, then we can gain perspective on ourselves. And just as valuable is the perspective offered from within by the unconscious, which confronts us with the otherness of its contradictory feelings, surprising fantasies, and nighttime dreams. *"What we see in the mirror held up to us by the [unconscious],"* Marie-Louise von Franz wrote, *"is hence the only source of genuine self-knowledge*; everything else is only narcissistic rumination of the ego about itself."[34]

Narcissus did not and could not love himself, because he did not know himself. What he loved instead was a superficial, cartoonish representation of who he was. "Poor foolish boy," Ovid commented, "why vainly grasp at the fleeting image that eludes you? … What you see is but the shadow cast by your reflection; in itself it is nothing."[35] But if we can step out of the spell of narcissism, we can be more open to otherness inside and outside of us, enjoying more genuine ways of relating to people and embracing a more complex, richer picture of ourselves.

Notes

1. Grimm and Grimm, *The Grimm Reader*, 167.
2. Grimm and Grimm, *The Grimm Reader*, 296.
3. Grimm and Grimm, *The Grimm Reader*, 297.
4. One reason why fairy tales stand apart within literature is that they do not have an identified author, but instead they emerged over time, as generations of oral storytellers have worked and reworked themes and characters into the canon. It is these collective bases that make them candidates for endless psychological interpretations. A study on the Grimms and the folk and fairy tales they collected is Tatar, *Grimms' Fairy Tales*. Maria Tatar also presented interpretative approaches used

by historians, literary critics, folklorists, cultural anthropologists, and psychoanalysts of many different schools of thought.
5. A classic reference on the Jungian interpretation of fairy tales is von Franz, *Interpretation of Fairy Tales*.
6. Jungian psychological interpretations of this tale have been proposed by Seifert, *Snow White*, Takenaka, "Realization of Absolute Beauty," and Dougherty, "Snow White."
7. When the Grimms realized that their collection was being read not just by adults, but by children as well, and being eager for bigger royalties, they decided to cater more directly to younger readers. Hence, they decided to rewrite some of the tales in their collection to reduce the amount of sex and to increase the amount of violence—a remarkable pedagogical approach. The Grimms also wanted to refrain from casting parents as abusive or evil in their revised editions: enter stepparents, who now took the blame for everything evil. See Tatar, *Grimms' Fairy Tales*.
8. Grimm and Grimm, *The Grimm Reader*, 168.
9. Grimm and Grimm, *The Grimm Reader*, 168.
10. Grimm and Grimm, *The Grimm Reader*, 172.
11. Grimm and Grimm, *The Grimm Reader*, 176.
12. For this satirical poem and its rendition of femininity, and for his positions expressed both in public and in private, Swift has been called a misogynist. An in-kind rebuttal of his "The Lady's Dressing Room" was given by Lady Mary Wortley Montagu in her poem "The Reasons that Induced Dr S to Write a Poem Call'd the Lady's Dressing Room." Written in 1734, it ends with an invitation to Swift, "I'm glad you'l write, You'l furnish paper when I shite." We will explore later the redeeming quality of humor whenever we are in the deadening hold of ideals of perfection and grandiosity.
13. Ovid, *Metamorphoses* 3.334ff. Translated by Mary M. Innes (London: Penguin Books, 1955).
14. Ovid, *Metamorphoses* 3.334ff.
15. Ovid, *Metamorphoses* 3.368ff.
16. Ovid, *Metamorphoses* 3.405ff.
17. Ovid, *Metamorphoses* 3.443ff.
18. These are the versions of the myth by Konon and by Parthenius; in these, a Narcissus flower springs from his blood.
19. Mario Jacoby asserted that the term "primary narcissism" may not well describe the original state of bliss. The term narcissism seems to imply, he argued, a separate individual who tries to control and dominate the other. Instead in infancy, Jacoby and many other authors have argued, children do not perceive parents and others as separate, but instead live fused and immersed in a sustaining, undifferentiated whole, which includes child and parents. See Jacoby, *Individuation and Narcissism*, 32–5.

The definition of narcissism as a needed and healthy phase in the development of children is mostly linked to the theories put forward by Heinz Kohut. In his opinion, healthy narcissism is specifically linked to the emergence of ambitions, self-esteem, and ideals. I have expounded some of his ideas in chapter 2. It is worth noting here that he often used the terms grandiosity and narcissism interchangeably, while I argue that distinguishing them is useful. An excellent review of Kohut's ideas is Siegel, *Kohut*.

For a thorough review of the concept of narcissism in its various reinterpretations, with a particular focus on relating Kohut's self-psychology and Jungian psychology, see Jacoby, *Individuation and Narcissism*. A collection of foundational papers on narcissism is Morrison, *Essential Papers on Narcissism*. A Jungian approach to narcissism is Schwartz-Salant, *Narcissism and Character Transformation*.

20. Kernberg, "Factors in the Psychoanalytic Treatment of Narcissistic Personalities," in Morrison, *Essential Papers on Narcissism*, 213–4.
21. Ovid, *Metamorphoses* 3.368ff.
22. Ovid, *Metamorphoses* 3.368ff. Winnicott wrote, "The man who falls in love with beauty is quite different from the man who loves a girl and feels she is beautiful and can see what is beautiful about her." Winnicott, *Playing and Reality*, 152.
23. Ovid, *Metamorphoses* 3.368ff.
24. While therapists may be tempted to perennially echo or be silent in session—to create "space" for their patients, but also as a way to avoid conflict—these are rarely therapeutic. West wrote, "While the analyst does have to be sensitively aware of the impact of their comments, it is not the case that the analyst should necessarily act to avoid the introduction of separateness. Indeed, helping the patient work through the experience of the analyst's difference is one of the key elements of the process of analysis." *Feeling, Being, and Self*, 79. Symington similarly wrote, "If I allow myself to get in a situation where a patient acts in such a way that I am shut out (and of course I represent the other), then the narcissism will remain untouched." *Narcissism*, 65–6.
25. Symington wrote, "the core of narcissism is a hatred of the relational." *Narcissism*, 18. A quote attributed to Kernberg is that narcissists are "envious of everything, even of other people's object relations." See Miller, "Depression and Grandiosity as Related Forms of Narcissistic Disturbances," in Morrison, *Essential Papers on Narcissism*, 330. To be relational, one has to see others as separate people, and so to accept, even embrace, differences.
26. West wrote of an "affective appraisal mechanism" that "is understood to consistently appraise experience in terms of the *sameness and difference* with/from/to the individual's developing set of preferences." *Feeling, Being, and Self*, xvii. West links the affective appraisal mechanism to a number of functions: "perception, classification, and appraisal; relating, self-regulation, and affect regulation; distinguishing self from other and developing a picture of the self; orienting the individual to the world; developing a picture of the relations between self and other; generating a sense of being; structuring experiences of infinite affect; and providing the primary link to reality." *Feeling, Being, and Self*, 11.
27. Whenever we reject what is within us, whenever we try to suppress feelings and thoughts, these unwanted parts of ourselves never really disappear. Instead, they return with stronger—and darker—energy. It is this repression of otherness that fuels the paranoid feelings often observed in narcissism. This paranoia reappears as an inner critic, a self-critical inner voice which makes narcissistic strivings of dominion over otherness doomed to fail; if nothing else, because the critical voice is always present as an unwanted other. In projection, the paranoia shows as the feeling that people are critical, hostile, shallow, or uncaring—making whatever is left of relationships utterly unsatisfying.
28. All the same, just because something is common, even universal, it does not mean that it is healthy. We may all have a measure of narcissism, but those of us less prone to narcissistic ways of relating do not need to work on becoming *less* accepting of differences. If one can move flexibly between sameness and difference, does not feel threatened by what is perceived as other, and is accepting of the many parts that constitute their psychology, that seems pretty good already. See Symington, *Narcissism*, 8–9.

29. Myths are rich in metaphors and symbols, and Narcissus' myth is no exception. Many different psychological interpretations have been offered for it; for instance, Jacoby identified as its central theme the ambivalent gift of self-knowledge, which is both painful and liberating, and that brings upon transformation. See Jacoby, *Individuation and Narcissism*, 17.
30. The Jungian analyst Rushi Ledermann, for instance, wrote that narcissistic disorder stems from the "catastrophically bad fit between the baby and the mother"; with needs for love and attunement left unmet, she argued, children build a pseudo-independence and grandiosity that does away with relationships, "Narcissistic Disorder and Its Treatment," 303. Mothers caught in all-encompassing attempts to satisfy their own psychological needs, argued instead the psychoanalyst Alice Miller, cannot relate to their children as emerging separate people. Subsequently, their children—especially those who happen to be very attuned to the emotional states of their mothers, being "gifted" with sensitive relational antennas—never know themselves and in turn display the same narcissistic focus of their mothers. See Miller, *Gifted Child*.

    Compare with Jacoby, who writes "nearly all my analysands suffering from a narcissistic disorder told me that their mother had been, in her own way, very 'devoted' to her children." *Individuation and Narcissism*, 134. The mother's fault is different—for Jacoby it is over-involvement—but the responsibility seems to stay. In my experience with narcissistic patients, I found that some of their mothers really seemed unemphatic and withdrawn, possibly because of depression, narcissism, or substance use, but others had mothers who were quite loving and caring, although often spurned by my patients. There is little determinism in psychological development.
31. Symington also wrote of the alternative choice, which is to turn toward the other and in this way embrace what he called the "lifegiver." He described the lifegiver as a part of ourselves, a symbol of vitality and otherness at once. Symington, *Narcissism*.
32. Winnicott, *Playing and Reality*, 149.
33. Winnicott also argued that if mothers are depressed, overwhelmed, or distracted, then when their children look at them, they will only see their mothers' own struggles. Lacking accurate mirroring, Winnicott wrote, "they look and they do not see themselves." *Playing and Reality*, 151.
34. von Franz, *Projection and Re-Collection*, 187. Her italics; I have substituted her word "Self" with "unconscious," for ease of understanding. von Franz refers to the Self as to "the center of the unconscious and of the whole psyche." von Franz, *Projection and Re-Collection*, 187. Her book offers an exploration of the nature of mirrors and mirroring within the framework of Jungian psychology.
35. Ovid, *Metamorphoses* 3.405ff.

References

Dougherty, N. "Snow White." In *Vol. 3 of Psyche's Stories: Modern Jungian Interpretations of Fairy Tales*, edited by M. Stein and L. Corbett, 65–80. Wilmette, Illinois: Chiron, 1995.

Grimm, J. and Wilhelm G. *The Grimm Reader: The Classic Tales of the Brothers Grimm*. Translated by Maria Tatar. New York: W.W. Norton & Company, 2010.

Jacoby, M. *Individuation and Narcissism: The Psychology of Self in Jung and Kohut*. Oxford: Routledge, 2017. First published 1990.

Ledermann, R. "Narcissistic Disorder and Its Treatment," *Journal of Analytical Psychology* 27, 1985, 202–321.

Miller, A. *The Drama of the Gifted Child: The Search for the True Self.* Rev. ed. New York: Basic Books, 1997.

Morrison, A. P., ed. *Essential Papers on Narcissism.* New York: New York University, 1986.

Schwartz-Salant, N. *Narcissism and Character Transformation: The Psychology of Narcissistic Character Disorders.* Toronto, Canada: Inner City Books, 1982.

Seifert, T. *Snow White.* Wilmette, Illinois: Chiron, 1986.

Siegel, A. M. *Heinz Kohut and the Psychology of the Self.* Hove, England: Brunner-Routledge, 1996.

Symington, N. *Narcissism: A New Theory.* London: Karnac, 1993.

Takenaka, N. "The Realization of Absolute Beauty: An Interpretation of the Fairytale Snow White," *Journal of Analytical Psychology* 61(4), 2016, 497–514.

Tatar, M. *The Hard Facts on the Grimms' Fairy Tales.* 2nd ed. Princeton: Princeton University Press, 2003.

von Franz, M.-L. *Projection and Re-Collection in Jungian Psychology: Reflections of the Soul.* Chicago and La Salle, Illinois: Open Court, 1980.

von Franz, M.-L. *The Interpretation of Fairy Tales.* Rev. ed. Boulder: Shambhala, 1996.

West, M. *Feeling, Being, and the Sense of Self: A New Perspective on Identity, Affect, and Narcissistic Disorders.* London: Karnac Books, 2007.

Winnicott, D. W. *Playing and Reality.* Oxon: Routledge, 2002. First published 1971.

8

STORIES OF ALTRUISM, MORALITY, VICTIMHOOD—AND DELUSIONS

The pursuit of "the greater good" has always been an uncertain enterprise. For one, the expression itself—the greater good—has been used to convey different ideas. In the context of war, for example, it refers to the sacrifices that are imposed on some people, at times even their deaths, for the supposed benefit of a larger group, like their country. In this case, the greater good is invoked to make palatable those courses of action that would otherwise be morally questionable. Other times, the greater good is the motivating principle of people who care deeply about others and society and who make altruistic choices even when they entail personal sacrifices. It would be cliché—and based on our own envy—to claim that their altruism is not genuine, that those who pursue the greater good are always motivated by some other, hidden, self-serving agenda. But at least some of the time, the pursuit of the greater good and of any virtue—altruism, empathy, modesty—can be hijacked by grandiosity, that is by dreams of impossible, uncompromising, and extraordinary virtues. In this chapter, we explore how our higher, loftier goals could actually originate from a set of conflicting motivations.[1]

For "the well-being of mankind," the charitable Rosenwald Fund was created by the Chicago businessman Julius Rosenwald in 1917. Rosenwald established himself as an owner of Sears, which he built into the great merchandise retailer it once was, the largest in the United States for many decades; then, he turned to philanthropy. Aware that foundations can become bureaucratic and ultimately ineffectual, Rosenwald gave a mandate that his fund disburse all its assets within 25 years after his death—an unusual choice among wealthy philanthropists, who may have preferred their names be celebrated for eternity. In a recent biography, the historian Hasia Diner quipped, "He had no interest in slapping his name on buildings, no desire to see it boldly projected on public spaces"—a sense of modesty he carried throughout his philanthropic life.[2]

Among the many institutions and causes he supported, Rosenwald was passionate about the advancement of black people in America, from urban centers to the rural South—a passion that brought him into partnership with the prominent leader Booker T. Washington. By the end of his life in 1932, the Rosenwald Fund had financed fellowships, created a network of libraries, and opened more than 5,000 schools, which at one point enrolled more than one-third of black children in the South.

The Rosenwald Fund also promoted public health initiatives for black Americans. At the beginning of the twentieth century, the American health system was mostly based on private medicine and fee-for-service—many, and not just the poorest, effectively did not have access to healthcare. The Rosenwald Fund tackled some of these needs with initiatives that today might be called community medicine, with the added explicit goal of improving race relations. Among these innovative initiatives, some addressed the epidemic of syphilis.

Now curable by antibiotics, in the pre-penicillin era syphilis was widespread and dangerous. For those who could afford it, there was treatment available that promised to limit contagiousness, slow down progression, and even cure the disease—a treatment that relied on arsenic derivatives and heavy metals. For most people, and disproportionately so for black Americans in the South, treatment remained inaccessible.

One federal agency tasked with the promotion of the greater good was the Public Health Service (PHS). Its Division of Venereal Diseases addressed these needs by promoting health programs, but their initiatives focused on urban populations, and their funding was modest. To provide syphilis prevention and treatment programs to rural areas and black communities, the Rosenwald Fund and the PHS decided to partner in 1930. In keeping with Rosenwald's commitment to ameliorating race relations, the Rosenwald Fund required that any joint program would entail culturally-appropriate health services, train and hire black nurses and physicians, and create non-segregated workplaces.

Perhaps surprisingly, this was the beginning of the now infamous Tuskegee Study.[3] It is in the city of Tuskegee, Alabama, that the PHS and the Rosenwald Fund joined forces with the black Tuskegee Institute, local government, and physicians' organizations to provide a one-year community outreach program on syphilis. It was called a "syphilis control demonstration," which, if successful, could be replicated across the country.[4] The demonstration entailed community screenings (via blood tests) for syphilis and, for those diagnosed with the disease, one year of free treatment.[5] At the conclusion of the planned year, the demonstration was deemed a success. Thousands of people were screened and treated, many of whom had never seen a doctor before. Governmental agencies and private philanthropy had worked well together, showing that public health initiatives could be successful in the field.

One wonders then how such a progressive public health initiative turned into the infamous "Tuskegee Study of Untreated Syphilis in the Negro Male," as it was called—a study that lasted for 40 more years. When the planned one-year demonstration was over, the physicians at the PHS proposed that the Rosenwald Fund extend it. Now struggling in the post-Depression years, the Rosenwald Fund could not commit to a longer or broader initiative, and so it ended its involvement with the Tuskegee initiative, waiting for better times to advance its public health projects. With the financial backing of the Rosenwald Fund gone, the officials at the PHS refused to give up what they called an "unparalleled opportunity." They decided to continue the initiative in Tuskegee, but this time as a "scientific" study where they would follow the progression of syphilis without providing any treatment.

They identified 399 black men, who were not told and did not consent to be in a research experiment. Neither were they told they had syphilis and so were potentially contagious. Instead, they were only falsely told they had "bad blood," and that the doctors of the PHS were treating the disease for free. On top of this, these men became unable to access any doctors in their hometown, as local physicians were asked to deny them care. Even when penicillin finally became available as a cure for syphilis, the PHS made the decision to continue the study, withholding this form of treatment too.[6]

The Tuskegee Study ultimately ran until 1972, handed down from one generation of physicians to the next within the PHS. It was never a secret study, as research articles about the men, their declining health, and mortality rates appeared over decades on reputable peer-reviewed medical journals. The morality of the study itself was never questioned by those involved, and neither were its underpinning racism, classism, and paternalism. It was only when whistleblowers and journalists brought attention to this immoral program that a public scandal ensued, bringing the tragic study to an end with apologies by the government and eventually a court victory for the survivors and their families.

While we can only speculate about the motivations of those who carried out the Tuskegee Study, letters, memos, and meeting minutes from the PHS archives offer glimpses of their goals and pursuits.[7] The officers and physicians of the PHS were moved by dreams of fame and professional prestige. There had been a widely cited study—called the Oslo Study—documenting the effects of untreated syphilis on a group of white men in Norway—a study that brought accolades to its investigators. Many in the medical field had debated whether syphilis affected whites and blacks differently, a debate informed by an ongoing obsession with racial differences. In Tuskegee, the PHS physicians found an opportunity to run a parallel study on black people—"a perfect gold mine" of new data, one wrote— that would have brought recognition to their names.[8] One officer said that he was "confident that the results of this study, if anywhere near our expectations, will attract world wide attention."[9] Another foretellingly wrote, "It will either cover us with mud or glory when completed."[10]

A distorted pursuit of the greater good also shaped their thinking. For one, the PHS officials thought that the study was advancing medical knowledge, "for the sake of humanity," as a nurse said.[11] And by learning about the disease in black people specifically, the physicians argued that they were improving their medical treatment and even overall race relations. As the historian James Jones wrote about the PHS officials who started the Tuskegee Study,

> [They] devoted their careers to eradicating syphilis. ... [They] called themselves "syphilis men," so great was their identification with their jobs. *They were crusaders, true believers.* ... Their efforts established the pattern for the national campaign that [the PHS] launched a few years later when, once again, mobile clinics were dispatched in the South [offering treatment to black people]. ... [They] promoted black hiring ... [and] advanced medical training in the nation's leading medical schools for older black staff members. In short, the PHS officials behind the Tuskegee Study were racial liberals by the standards of the 1930s. Within the medical profession, they were truly progressive. They began the experiment because they were interested in black health, in studying the effects of syphilis on black people.[12]

And yet, as Jones denounced in his 1981 exposé of the Tuskegee Study, the physicians were unfazed by their plan to (supposedly) improve medical treatment by withholding available treatment from the men in the Study. Incredibly, they espoused the definition of the greater good used in war, arguing it moral to impose sacrifices on the few for the sake of the rest of us. In 1951, 20 years into the Study, they argued that *stopping* their experiment would be immoral. Despite being aware that their investigation "contributed to [the men's] ailments," the physicians paternalistically stated: "we have a high moral obligation to those who have died to make this the best study possible." They felt a responsibility to prove to the men that "their willingness to serve"—a willingness never ascertained—"to serve, even at the risk of shortening their lives, as experimental subjects" was not in vain.

This is grandiose morality—the grandiosity of determining what is right not only for oneself but also for others, irrespective of their own wishes. Grandiose morality leads us to believe that we know with certainty what the greater good is, doing away with ethical dilemmas. It was this grandiosity that transformed a sound public health initiative into a tragic experiment—an experiment from which, as a PHS physician concluded in 1970, "nothing learned will prevent, find, or cure a single case of infectious syphilis."[13]

More recently, the physician David Feldshuh wrote a play titled *Susceptible to Kindness* about the Tuskegee Study, for which he became a 1992 finalist for the Pulitzer Prize for Drama. Reportedly, Feldshuh became interested in understanding the Tuskegee story as he wondered if he too may unwittingly be part of grand clinical and research projects that years later could be exposed as immoral. With Feldshuh, we may wonder if our pursuits may be expressions of grandiosity, including when we think we are working to do good.

◆

I remember back when I was in college, passionate about politics and economic reform. It was just before the year 2000, which the Catholic Church had declared a Jubilee year, a year of forgiveness and indulgence (in the religious sense of the word, of course). Based on the biblical imperative of forgiving debts, a social campaign had emerged to advocate for the cancellation of debt for the world's poorest countries. When a prominent Italian politician, a leader of the party I had campaigned for, came to our campus in Bologna to support the debt-forgiveness campaign, my classmates and I went to attend his lecture.

His talk puzzled me, however, because of his tone and remarks. He was a charming, brilliant man, who ended up discussing the topics of poverty and famine with such flippant lightness: witty jokes about the singer Bono of the band U2—Bono being a speaker for the debt relief campaign—odd comments about African countries' negotiating skills, and attacks on his political opponents. More than a presentation on poverty and its remedies, it seemed like a late-night talk show, meant to highlight only the brilliance of the politician himself. The audience felt excited and laughed along; after all, we were supposedly "on the right side of history," as he said, congratulating each other on our moral and political rightfulness. With the terminology I later learned studying psychology, one could say that his affect was incongruent—the seriousness of the topic and his supposed moral indignation were not matched by his demeanor.

Even more crushing for my naiveté was the conversation I had with him just below the podium after his lecture. I was eager to apply the tools I was learning in my economics program, and brought him questions on how to be sure that debt forgiveness would have lasting impact, and how to guarantee access to credit markets in the years following the cancellation… With a broad smile and a gesture of his hand, he interrupted me. "You know," he said with reassuring voice, "the debts we are forgiving are 'bad debts,' they are debts that would not have been repaid anyway. This initiative will not have a large impact on these countries' economies." I was stunned—"So what is the point of forgiving them?" He nonchalantly replied, "It is good that people mobilize, that they become involved in such an important topic." That the proposed solution may have had only minimal impact did not faze him.

These convoluted rationalizations signal that we have lost touch with our genuine sense of morality. Ethical dilemmas are now being dismissed with self-serving shortcuts. We start considering our actions and motivations above the need for scrutiny, so sure we are of our stances. And when grandiosity takes morality hostage, we come to believe that choices, lifestyles, and values are either right or wrong—and that we are on the right side, of course. The tone of our strivings shifts from inspirational to pedantic, and morality becomes moralism. We loudly declare what is appropriate, decent, and just. Then, we erect an impeccable and virtuous persona, an image that hides and denies all our inevitable contradictions, missteps, doubts, ambivalence, and ever-present selfish needs. We become exhibitionists of our alleged virtues. And if we receive any feedback on our rigidity or on the inconsistencies between our words and actions—even just from friends humoring us—we become defensive, so invested we are in maintaining our moral status.

As an example, I am reminded of a young couple I knew. They both were committed to the environment. Accordingly, they contributed to environmental initiatives, donating their money and time, and pursued careers in the field. But the couple also took it upon themselves to constantly educate their friends and family on their wasteful lifestyles, while describing, may I say celebrating, how they had adjusted their own lives in accord with their nature-conscious values. It seemed to me, however, that they were missing a few contradictions here and there. They criticized mass tourism and so would only vacation in "green" resorts, but these were often located a couple of intercontinental flights away from where they lived. When they decided to upgrade their living quarters, they asked a LEED-certified architect how to make it environmentally friendly; however, it was a seven-bedroom mansion for their household of two. One of them was proud to say that she never walked on grass, so as not to damage it. I shared with her that prairies benefit from yearly fires.

The specific virtues that we extol do not matter; any virtue can be elevated by our grandiose strivings. Some embrace the virtues of success and money; others celebrate altruism and modesty. Some focus on the virtues of monogamy or even abstinence from "temptations of the flesh"; others explain that true liberation comes only from a sexuality without commitments. Religion is an obvious fertile terrain for moralism, but so are social activism, environmentalism, psychological theories, and politics, among many others.

What is denied within ourselves is then projected onto others. "We are wholly good," we say, "while they are flawed, selfish, naive, unreasonable, sinful, or uncivilized." The hallmark of grandiose virtues is the "holier than thou" stance, the ongoing comparisons that imply that there is always an other who is inferior to us, so that *our* morality can shine. Even worse, we may feel that it is our job to sternly impart our goodness onto others, and we become preachy and paternalistic.

The caricatures we make of other people, if we are curious and humble enough, most clearly show which aspects of our personality we are uncomfortable with. Alas, it is easier to judge somebody out there, than to become aware of those rejected sides of ourselves. There are just too many examples of male preachers, priests, and politicians who for decades were crusaders against homosexuality and who later found themselves caught in some gossipy scandal involving sex with other men, often and sadly consumed in inappropriate professional settings, skewed power dynamics, or airport bathrooms. One wonders if the vehemence of their preaching is proportional to the intensity of their own disavowed desires.

For other people, grandiosity is rooted in their experience of having been hurt. I do not intend to dismiss the reality of pain, both physical and emotional, and its pervasive effects. Our experiences, especially those that are scary and hurtful, leave behind anxieties, fears, sadness, and grief that can accompany us for a long time, and sometimes for life. These painful experiences are part of our history and identity—their memory a testament of love lost, broken plans, injustice, and the unpredictability of life.

However, hurt can be hijacked by grandiose wishes to be special, leading to victimhood. Feeling rejected in life, some may seek to reestablish balance by claiming moral superiority over those who rejected them; they may identify with the virtues of the martyrs. For instance, a breakup may be a hurtful experience for both partners; however, the one who did not initiate it usually assumes some moral superiority as a way to soften the blow, saying things like "I would have tried harder," or "It was her fear of commitment." When faced by painful experiences, some people may react by grandiosely affirming their own pure, innocent nature versus the hurtful, uncaring other. But just because we were hurt in one situation does not mean that we might not be the ones hurting others at the next juncture. Some people may respond with moral indignation even when there is no one to blame for their pain, directing their complaints and entitlement toward whomever comes within reach.

During a group therapy session in a hospital, noticing the dryness of her hands, a therapist took lotion out of her purse. Without thinking anything of it, she was moved to share it with the person next to her, and so this lotion passed from patient to patient in the sitting circle. When the lotion finally reached a woman with a skin condition (akin to an allergy or rash), this woman became appalled. She could not put anything on her skin, she shared resentfully, and yet the therapist, well aware of her skin condition, had nevertheless passed it around for everyone to use except her. Because she could not use the lotion, she seemed to believe, everyone should go without it. And in the indignation of being singled out, declaring out loud the perceived lapse in the therapist's empathy, she made herself morally superior and so, special.

At the core of victimhood, there may be an unconscious fantasy of rewinding time and undoing the past. There is a Buddhist story that manages to be compassionate, while challenging the claim that our pain—even when it is the worst pain imaginable—is special, rather than part of the totality of life. In the story, a mother's only son had suddenly died and, struck with grief, she carried him around for days asking for somebody who could bring him back to life—a grandiose, impossible wish. Those who she encountered offered sympathy and support, but she kept looking for the one person who could actually cure her dead son. She finally met a Buddhist monk, who told her that he would heal the boy. To make the medicine, he said, she needed to bring him a small bag filled with mustard seeds, with each seed donated by a family who had never experienced a death. Still carrying her son, she went from house to house, and everyone was willing to give her mustard seeds, but when asked if their families had ever been touched by death, they all shared a long list of deceased relatives. "The living are few," they each said, "but the dead are many." Unable to collect even one seed, she buried her son, accepted her grief, and returned to the monk to learn the Buddhist way. When we are able to embrace our hurt, we are freed from hopeless fantasies and the impossible requests we make of others. Rather than being isolated in our pain, we open up to the opportunities for support and community that may arise.

Small injuries, too, can lead us to temporarily act out our victimhood. For some, a common cold becomes an occasion for petulance—we sound like children again as we ask our relatives to please open the windows, bring us food, buy us aspirin, or cancel our appointments for the day. The truth is that we can do all these things by ourselves, but for a day or so we feel entitled to special accommodations. And when our relatives oblige, we enjoy for a little while this very pleasurable regression, the fantasy of returning to the original blissful state of childhood—the time when we were tended to—a frame of mind that hopefully wanes as the fever abates.

If our victimhood becomes a longer-term deal, however, it can tire our friends and family. They may feel resentful for the litany of requests: that they drive us around because we do not have a car; that they do not mention their own happy marriages because we are single; that they listen again and again as we vent about our large collection of slights received. If we are caught by victimhood, we leave no space for our friends' lives and for *their* hurt. Over time, they may give up the expectation that the relationship will ever be reciprocal in care. Stuck in our own narratives of slights and loneliness, we may unwittingly end up pushing friends away, reinforcing the self-fulfilling prophecy of rejection.

While nonprofits used to be run by Executive Directors, nowadays many are switching to the trendier title Chief Executive Officer, apparently seeking the status and legitimacy of the corporate world. I worked with a college student who said she wanted to become the CEO of a nonprofit. "A nonprofit that does what?" I asked. Her answer was, "I don't know yet. What I know is that I want to run one." The title came before the mission, even as she shared with friends and family that she was primarily motivated by the pursuit of the greater good. Yet, through her dream to become CEO, she was able to find the energy to pursue her ambitions of professional success. Ambition and grandiosity, however, can take more extreme forms; they can become delusional and cause us to lose touch with reality.

Carl Jung discussed how the ego—our sense of who we are—can attach to the figures found in the unconscious and so become "inflated" with their status and power.[14] From time to time, we may grandiosely identify with larger-than-life figures such as the eternal lover, the hero, the magician, the king, the genius, the saint, or even the friend of God.[15] It happens whenever we succeed at something we value, for instance when we are admitted at our preferred college, win an athletic competition, or exchange a first kiss. We feel confident and brave, as if all possibilities are available to us, and we suddenly walk "five feet above the ground." The experiences that trigger inflation can also be more private ones, such as psychological or spiritual insight. For instance, we may be moved to tears by a sunset, feel deep self-love during a yoga class, or feel a rush of compassion when we forgive somebody. Experiences of boundless love and connection have been described in psychology as an "oceanic feeling," a description that well describes their felt magnitude. We forget for a moment our limitations and that we will soon have to "shrink" back to a more ordinary size. For a little while, we bask in the glory.

It is important, however, that we retain the ability to distinguish what is real from what is impossible or even absurd. The student who aspired to be a nonprofit CEO, for instance, was moved by images of success but remained well aware that she would have to make her way up the ladder with effort and time. Even when she became lost in daydreams—imagining herself speaking to large audiences at a yearly fundraiser gala "as if" she was a CEO—her fantasy was only a vision of what might be possible. When such thoughts would pass, she could distinguish facts from fiction; she knew that she was a student, not yet a community leader.

Whether because of drugs, genetics, life experiences, or psychological mindsets, some people do get stuck in such grandiose identifications, which can be isolating, problematic, or even dangerous. For them, identification with the figures of the unconscious "seizes hold of the psyche with a kind of primeval force and compels it to transgress the bounds of humanity," wrote Jung. The consequence is "a puffed-up attitude (inflation), loss of free will, delusion, and enthusiasm in good and evil alike."[16] For instance, I briefly worked with a young man who, in a manic state, had printed business cards at home. He gave me one, on which he had only written his name and CEO—no company was listed. Unlike my other patient, he had become lost in the power of grandiose images, literally believing himself to be somebody he was not—he had become delusional.

In the most dangerous cases of delusions, some may identify with evil figures, such as the devil or a notorious killer. These people are taken by grandiose fantasies of being powerful and invulnerable, and often seek to be known and remembered, even if only in the annals of evil. For instance, many young school shooters left behind detailed accounts of the real and perceived slights they experienced. But instead of grieving, they try to free themselves from their pain by seeking revenge and becoming pain itself—an undertaking destined to fail and result in tragedy for all. And in such distorted moral takes on the idea of "seeking justice," we most clearly observe the tremendous dangers of grandiosity left unchecked.

Notes

1. A recent book illustrating these conflicting motivations and the resulting rationalizations is Giridharadas, *Winners Take All*.
2. Diner, *Julius Rosenwald*, xi.
3. Detailed accounts of the Tuskegee Study, the racial discrimination that made it possible, and its impact on the American consciousness about race relations are Jones, *Bad Blood*, and Reverby, *Examining Tuskegee*.

4. The Public Health Service and the Rosenwald Fund also led additional demonstrations across six different States, treating a total of 40,000 black people.
5. Jones identified shortcomings even in this early phase of the demonstration. Due to paternalistic attitudes, for instance, the physicians did not educate those who tested positive for syphilis; as a result, many were not made aware of the sexually transmittable nature of their infection. Jones, *Bad Blood*, 72–4.
6. Contrary to popular belief, the physicians did not infect the men with syphilis; this study recruited people who already had the disease. This does not mean that the Public Health Service never infected people with syphilis as part of their research studies. In fact, in 1946 they infected inmates with syphilis, this time in Guatemala. While the inmates were at least given antibiotics, the physicians did not check that the treatment successfully cured the infection.
7. Jones first uncovered much of this documentation. His exposé *Bad Blood* was widely read. Jones was passionate about his research, as an historian and a social advocate, and he later joined forces with famed civil rights lawyer Fred Gray, who successfully sued the government for the Tuskegee Study.
8. A key difference between the two studies was that the Oslo Study was based on retrospective case histories of men who went to a hospital for treatment, not on the withholding of needed treatment for the purpose of observation. See also Jones, *Bad Blood*, 122.
9. Record of USPHS Venereal Disease Division, Record Group 90, National Archives, Washington National Record Center, Suitland, Maryland. As cited by Jones, *Bad Blood*, 112.
10. Jones, *Bad Blood*, 112.
11. Jones, *Bad Blood*, 169.
12. Jones, *Bad Blood*, 171–2. Italics are mine.
13. Incredibly, even this physician argued in favor of continuing the study due to having an "obligation" to the remaining patients. Jones, *Bad Blood*, 202.
14. These are the ever-present images and figures that emerge from what Jung called "archetypes," the "unconscious images of the instincts themselves." Jung, *Archetypes*, par 380*ff*. These archetypes "behave like highly charged autonomous centers of power" and "they exert a fascinating and possessive influence" upon the ego. Jung, *Psychology of the Unconscious*, par 110. "Inflation" and "grandiosity" are two terms to describe the same concept.
15. See Jung, *Psychology of the Unconscious*, par 377*ff*.
16. Jung, *Psychology of the Unconscious*, par 110.

References

Diner, H. R. *Julius Rosenwald: Repairing the World*. New Haven, Connecticut: Yale University Press, 2017.

Giridharadas, A. *Winners Take All: The Elite Charade of Changing the World*. New York: Knopf, 2018.

Jones, J. H. *Bad Blood: The Tuskegee Syphilis Experiment*. New and expanded ed. New York: The Free Press, 1993.

Jung, C. G. *On the Psychology of the Unconscious*. In *Two Essays in Analytical Psychology*. Vol. 7 of *The Collected Works of C. G. Jung*, edited by H. Read, M. Fordham, G. Adler and W. McGuire. Translated by R. F. C. Hull. 2nd ed. Princeton, NJ: Princeton University Press, 1972.

Jung, C. G. *The Archetypes and the Collective Unconscious*. In Vol. 9, bk. 1 of *The Collected Works of C. G. Jung*, edited by H. Read, M. Fordham, G. Adler, and W. McGuire. Translated by R. F. C. Hull. 2nd ed. Princeton, NJ: Princeton University Press, 1968.

Reverby, S. M. *Examining Tuskegee: The Infamous Syphilis Study and Its Legacy*. Chapel Hill, North Carolina: The University of North Carolina Press, 2009.

PART III
Callings

9
GRANDIOSITY AS A CALLING

> For some people the day comes
> When they have to declare the great Yes
> Or the great No.
>
> C. P. Cavafy, *Che fece ... il gran rifiuto*

"Go to the great city of Nineveh," the Biblical prophet Jonah was told by his God.[1] Words like "vocation" and "calling" are used nowadays mostly in the context of career choices, for instance, to describe someone's interest and passion for a job: "Becoming a teacher was his calling." Yet, the original meaning of these words is more literal: the prophets, and those who followed their example, were directly called by the gods—*vocatus* is Latin for "called"—and commanded to follow their demands.

The prophets were not always eager to comply; some were reluctant prophets. Answering their call, in fact, required sacrifices they might not have been willing to make, at least not without some convincing. For instance, when Jonah heard his calling, he ran away, toward Joppa. There, he found a ship and "sailed for Tarshish to flee from the Lord."[2] He was not on the run for long; a storm caught his ship and threatened to sink it. Jonah understood that to placate the stormy weather, he had to jump in the open water and surrender to God, and so he did. Swallowed and hence rescued by a big fish, he remained in its belly for three days, until he was spewed onto a beach. Upon being called a second time by God, Jonah went at once to Nineveh, this time without delay or hesitation. His previous experience fleeing the call turned out to be persuasive.

We do not have to be religious or believe in God to experience callings. We may feel "as if" we are being called upon whenever we fall into a "pocket" of grandiosity. Grandiose fantasies stir us and have power over us. They direct our actions, energize us, exhaust us, exalt our feelings, and at times even frighten us. Our reactions to these experiences—from elation to fear—are all reasonable. After all, grandiosity can lead us to great heights, but also painful disasters—surely not all of them worth sacrificing for. Like Jonah, we may decide to flee the opposite way—and sometimes that may be for the better.[3]

And among our grandiose fantasies, we may identify some that are deeply meaningful to us. These grandiose fantasies point us toward *pursuits that give our lives a sense of personal meaning and purpose*, and so I call them "callings." This definition of callings is meant to be psychological, rather than religious—it neither requires nor is incompatible with having religious beliefs. This second half of this book is dedicated to the task of identifying and pursuing our callings.

Some people may dismiss the need to identify their callings. They may incorrectly believe that their callings are simply what they want. They may declare, "I was born to be President," or "I know I am destined to be the next Steve Jobs"—statements that sound like ego trips. And, nowadays, there are many psychological and self-help approaches—and even some spiritual ones—that suggest people search their "why" and identify their values, so that they can live in alignment with them.

While these reminders to explore our motivations can be useful, we risk restating only the values and wishes of the ego itself. Rather than finding out what is actually driving us, we end up describing what we would like to be driven by. Indeed, when people are asked to identify their values, they tend to list things like courage, altruism, integrity, or perseverance. By looking at these lists of positive traits, one would get the impression that nobody is driven by less appealing motivations like greed, power, or lust. But these destructive motivations are the ones we would benefit from acknowledging the most, so that we do not mindlessly act them out.

The bottom line is that we cannot trust the ego alone when it comes to identifying our callings. We need to explore the totality of our motivations and grandiose fantasies, including the unconscious ones. We need to look beyond the wishes of our egos, which are so focused on control and their own self-preservation. We need to be open to pursuits we never considered before. We need to allow for new ideas about the world and ourselves. Frustrating our narcissistic desires for sameness, our callings push us toward new territories, possibly new heights, and well outside our comfort zone. And by setting us on our personal paths, our callings often also collide with the socially endorsed values of our time.

♦

The eleventh child of a family of farmers, Pietro da Morrone entered religious life as a young man.[4] In 1241, due to his love of solitude, he went to live in the wilderness of the heights of Mountain Morrone, from which he took his name, and later moved to even more isolated mountains in the Abruzzo region. Dwelling in caves, for years he lived an ascetic life that was rich in prayer, fasting, silence, and simplicity. Later, having gathered a following of people drawn to his life of privation and religiosity, he founded a new order of monks and managed to have it recognized by the hierarchies of the Catholic Church. His order, later named the Celestines, grew to 36 monasteries during his lifetime. His increasing popularity did not prevent him from seeking isolation again, choosing to retire in the mountains in his old age. But soon, the world he had left behind reclaimed him.

Split among religious and political factions, each loyal to a different European monarch, the medieval Catholic Church was a hub of power and wealth. After the death of the pope in 1292, infighting among the cardinals thwarted any attempt to elect a new pope for more than two years. Compelled to reach a compromise, the cardinals finally elected as pope a man with an impeccable reputation—already considered a saint during his lifetime—Pietro da Morrone. Allegedly, when a delegation of Vatican dignitaries ascended the mountain and shared with Pietro that he had been called to lead the Church, he initially fled, unwilling to renounce his secluded life.

He was crowned in the city of Aquila, where he arrived riding on a donkey—a sign of humility—and took the name Pope Celestine V. Many of his contemporaries hoped that he would renew the Church, moving it away from the materialistic concerns it had been consumed by. And at first, Celestine seemed to fulfill these hopes of renewal. For instance, in a clear break with the then common Catholic practice of forgiveness in exchange for money, Celestine granted free forgiveness to all pilgrims who would visit the Church of Santa Maria di Collemaggio in Aquila at the end of August, the anniversary of his crowning. His initiative was later widened with the establishment of Jubilee years of forgiveness, including the one in the year 2000 that I mentioned earlier.

In spite of the widespread hope of renewal he evoked, or perhaps because of it, his papacy did not last long. Pressured—some said manipulated—by various competing monarchs, unable to manage the intricacies of the Church bureaucracy and politics, and overwhelmed by it all, Celestine resigned after only five short months of papacy. He declared to the cardinals that his decision was for "the sake of humility, of a better life, and a stainless conscience, for the weakness of my body and my lack of knowledge, for the malignity of the people, for my personal infirmity, and to recover the tranquility of my former life."[5] He fled a second time toward his mountains, and supposedly later tried to sail away across the Adriatic Sea. Instead, he was apprehended and jailed for life by his eventual successor, Pope Boniface VIII, who probably feared that factions within the Church would make Celestine a leader of an opposing party, an antipope.

We too are most often caught among conflicting callings and fantasies, unsure of which we need to follow and which to flee. Celestine was drawn—by his contemporaries if not his God—to reform a Church in disarray. This was an earthly toil, an ambitious task that would have been fitting for a Sisyphus type, but for which Celestine was not willing or able to sacrifice his energy and peace of mind. Celestine was also called by his own spirituality to seek the contemplative life—a saintly life that better suited him, as he was likely a Puer type. Each grandiose fantasy had its value and costs, both for Celestine as a man and for society at large.

The poet Dante harshly judged Celestine's eventual choice, as he too had been hopeful for a renewal of the Church. Dante also had an ulterior reason for his ill feelings. Pope Boniface VIII, who succeeded Celestine after his resignation, was from a political faction opposed to Dante's. And for his political leanings, Dante was ultimately exiled from his native Florence, something he never forgave Celestine for. As Dante narrated his imaginary journey through the afterlife, he wrote of meeting Celestine, the one "who made the Great Refusal, impelled by cowardice"—*che fece per viltade il gran rifiuto*.[6] Dante attributed Celestine's resignation to cowardice and so placed him in the vestibule of Hell even though, after dying in the papal prisons, Celestine was actually (and ironically) proclaimed a saint.

Belonging to another family of Florentine exiles, the poet and scholar Petrarch had a different opinion of Celestine, considering him someone who "looking up towards the heavens, forgot the earth."[7] For Petrarch, Celestine was a person able to distinguish among competing duties and desires, resist social pressures, and remain true to his own individual calling. In his book *The Life of Solitude*, Petrarch admired Celestine's resignation as "the choice of an exalted and emancipated mind who knew no yoke and was truly celestial." In his view, Celestine recognized that the papacy was a "deadly burden" and was able to renounce it to live according to his own values. Quite the opposite of cowardice or selfishness, Celestine's resignation was seen as "good for him and the world, because the excessive heights he had reached could have been dangerous for all due to his lack of experience about human affairs, which he rejected for his contemplation of divine things."[8]

Ultimately, Celestine had to choose between political and ascetic heights, and he chose the latter. We are left with two opposing assessments of his renunciation—a coward or a hero—a contrast that Petrarch himself acknowledged noting that "people can have different, even opposite, opinions on any given topic due to the variety of their minds."[9]

◆

Callings open us up to new possibilities. They ignite transformations in the way we experience ourselves and relate to other people and the world. They elevate even the most ordinary tasks, illuminating them with a sense of purpose. And they give us mental energy to take risks, stepping out of our comfort zones. But if we flee them all, losing any sense of urgency, excitement, and drive, then we may not know what to do with our time and lives. Only watching TV shows—getting a little vicarious adrenaline—is not enough to sustain us. We have to engage directly with our callings.

Yet, as soon as we engage, we find ourselves caught by the many conflicting fantasies and expectations, unsure if we are being called or led astray. For instance, when thinking about whether we want to become parents, we may feel compelled to have children because raising them seems like a meaningful endeavor. At the same time, we may find ourselves drawn to grand undertakings that are in conflict with having children, such as the search for solitude, creative aims (like writing a book), or professional ventures that require much time and dedication. We may also feel coerced to have children by societal pressure, for instance when seeking the approval of our families and community. Variations of these conflicting desires emerge whenever we engage with major decisions, whether it be having children, caring for aging parents or a relative with disabilities, pursuing a promotion, retiring from work, changing careers, marrying, divorcing, pursuing social activism, or building financial security. Caught between incompatible wishes and multiple loyalties, we may find ourselves living a paradox—"damned if you do, damned if you don't."

While other people may have opinions and pass judgment on our potential paths, that should have little bearing on us. Their evaluations of our options can quickly become moralistic and based on convention. The fact is that from the outside, it is impossible for others to know what will be ultimately meaningful for us, and which sacrifices we will find worthwhile embracing. Due to the *variety of minds*, using Petrarch's words, people are going to find meaning in different paths. Identifying our callings is a personal task, which cannot be delegated.

The task that defines our lives is then to become aware of all of our grandiose fantasies, even if they pull us in many directions. Of course, we will not be able to—and neither would it be wise to—pursue them all, at least not when they present in those all-encompassing, compulsive forms. Yet, we can try to discern among them our callings, those paths that make us feel that what we do in our lives is personally relevant, exciting, and meaningful. Whatever paths we ultimately pursue, we will carry the burden of our choices, we will experience the inevitable sacrifices. But if we live in accordance with our callings, having a sense of direction and purpose, we may feel as if we have found the voice that summons us, like the prophets of old.

Notes

1. Jonah 1:1.
2. Jonah 1:3.
3. Carl Jung drew parallels between psychological development and religious callings; see Jung, *Development of Personality*. The Jungian psychologist James Hillman also proposed a psychological approach to callings in his *The Soul's Code*, a book that has informed the ideas presented here.
4. My main source on Morrone's life is in Italian: Golinelli, *Celestino V*.
5. Alfonso Chacon, Vitae et res gestae Pontificum Romanorum et S. R. E. Cardinalium ab initio nascentis Ecclesiae usque ad Clementem IX P. O. M., 1677.
6. Dante, *Inferno*, III, 59–60.
7. Petrarca, *De Vita Solitaria*, XXVI.

8. Petrarca, *De Vita Solitaria*, XXVI.
9. Petrarca, *De Vita Solitaria*, XXVI.

References

Golinelli, P. *Celestino V: Il Papa Contadino*. Milano, Italy: Mursia, 2007.
Hillman, J. *The Soul's Code: In Search of Character and Calling*. New York: Random House, 1996.
Jung, C. G. *The Development of Personality*. Vol. 17 of *The Collected Works of C. G. Jung*, edited by H. Read, M. Fordham, G. Adler, and W. McGuire. Translated by R. F. C. Hull. Princeton, NJ: Princeton University Press, 1954.

10

THE OPPOSITE OF GRANDIOSITY IS LAZINESS

We are all touched by grandiosity, at first through the imaginings of our childhood—fantasies that feed our creativity and self-esteem—and later in the competing grandiose fantasies of our adulthood. Notwithstanding the dangers and costs associated with them, our preoccupations with extraordinary achievements have the potential of highlighting our callings and infusing our lives with meaning and energy.

Some people, however, may be skeptical as to whether—to find a sense of purpose in life—we have to be animated by any grandiose fantasies at all. They may argue that we are more likely to find contentment if we renounce such exalted images and instead accept our lot. They may contend that most people never achieve anything extraordinary in their lives after all. Carl Jung himself suggested that the fullest realization of one's own psychological potential—what he called the development of the personality, or individuation—may be reserved for a minority of people who are able to embrace such an inebriating process—the search for one's own calling—without losing their footing in reality.[1] The examples provided in this book could also seem to support these views: biblical prophets, popes, heroes, and social reformers, among the others, may belong to a league which we do not. So, why would we ordinary folks try to relate to their lives and tribulations?

Before we too quickly dismiss the suggestion that we should become aware of our grandiose fantasies and even engage with some of them as our life callings, it is useful to consider what the polar opposite of grandiosity is. At first thought, one may think it is humility. But we already know that any virtue can become an exercise in grandiosity, and this includes the virtue of humility. Indeed, humility is often accompanied by a private arrogance, built on comparisons—the inner conviction that we are better than others, especially those "boastful" ones. "Although religions talk much of humility," writes the Jungian psychologist James

Hillman, "they do not tell us what it actually feels like except as a virtue, which is then no longer humility at all, but a new form of pride."[2] While on the surface humility is not accompanied by exhibitionism, often a humble façade is there to invite affirmations from those around us. Pointedly, the Israeli Prime Minister Golda Meir was reported to have said, "Don't be so humble. You aren't that great."

The opposite of grandiosity is instead laziness. Aversion toward work and lack of effort are some of its manifestations. More fundamentally, however, I am referring to laziness in the psychological realm as lack of concern—a paucity in character and values. We are lazy when we do not wrestle with our own fantasies and callings: when we neither embrace nor flee, but indolently ignore them to preserve our easy living and comfort.

"Without demerit and without praise"—*sanza 'nfamia e sanza lodo*.[3] This is how Dante described those who do not take a stance in their lives, who always remain uncommitted and neutral—and Dante placed Pope Celestine V among them. In his vision, they are rejected by Heaven and yet unwanted by Hell, their deeds not deserving of praise nor punishment. They just assemble together in the afterlife as an indistinct multitude—so large that Dante responded with astonishment to their number. As the scholar Tommaso Di Salvo wrote, their laziness was such that "they knew neither the sweetness of victory nor the bitterness of failure … they did not take an active and responsible role in their lives, but stayed at the margins."[4] Tellingly, Dante imagined them following a "whirling banner," a flag spinning around so quickly that nobody could actually see what was on it. In life and in death, they blindly followed goals and causes—the flag—that they did not understand and could not be moved to care for.

The world in which we live is shaped by complex social, political, economic, and psychological forces, bigger than any one person. And each of us is complex too, at times stuck in dysfunctional or destructive patterns that seem difficult to change. From time to time, however, we may have insight into how to better things, even just a fleeting intuition of what we can do differently and where it may lead. At these times, the question is whether we believe that change is possible and that we can have an impact; or else, we might let go of these fantasies, regarding them as impossible and naive, and instead accept the status quo.

If we decide to passively accept things as they are, then our grandiose fantasies disappear. Rather than imagining possibilities, we see reality through cynical and disillusioned lenses. What is the point of trying, we can catch ourselves thinking, when most marriages end in divorce, people only care about money, the system is rigged, voting is pointless, and our efforts always amount to nothing? What is the point of striving for new ways of relating given that people—including ourselves—never change? This way, we give up hope and lose faith. I have heard several patients share that they did not want to have children, afraid that they would pass to the next generation their struggles, either via their genes or their parenting. Having lost hope in transformations—those metamorphoses that Ovid described in his classic poem—my patients deemed change only an illusion; mere determinism had become their worldview.

It is in this disillusioned frame of mind that laziness and indolence take over. Our energy becomes absorbed by the inconsequential details of our lives, and our engagement with wider communities is limited to good intentions and proclamations—armchair quarterbacks on any topic. A cartoon by Liza Donnelly depicts two people leisurely chatting in a gym: "I didn't protest this war," one says to the other, "but I'll try to protest the next one." Internally, self-exploration comes to an end. We assert that there are no new insights about ourselves to be gained and so there is no point in digging deeper. We become passive, psychologically lazy. We give up the struggle with our grandiosity and miss all opportunities to become aware of our individual callings.

But something must still be guiding our lives, some orienting principle; if not our individual callings, then something else that gets us out of bed in the morning and through the days. If we succumb to psychological laziness, then what guides us is the conventional life. We borrow principles, maxims, values, and conventions from our surroundings—from mentors, peers, healers, celebrities, and advertisements, all the same. Rather than exploring our passions, we mindlessly follow the "whirling banner" of decorum, success, responsibility, moderation, and good taste—not as *we* define them, but as they are presented to us from the outside. As a patient of mine once said to me, "What I did in life was never my choice, but what I thought would be seen as reasonable." In other words, we live like everybody else seems to be living.

Among middle-class Americans, I have frequently heard the conventional life described as a predictable timeline. Eighteen-year-old teenagers should be eager to go to college in a different town, lest they remain emotionally attached to their parents. In their twenties, they can party, drink too much, and date without emotional attachment, while starting their ambitious careers. As their thirties approach, they promptly should be ready to marry. Then all their relatives ask them when the children—plural—are coming. Shortly after that, they can move to the suburbs—because they are safer places—and so on and so forth. This timeline may work well for some, but it does not have to be followed by all.

Yet many people seem to conform to these familial and cultural expectations, either mindlessly adopting them to fit in, or after having put up a little fight against them. And even when people express resentment toward these external forces shaping their lives, some actually may be relieved that they do not have to carve their own paths. The regrets, anxiety, or numbness resulting from compliance with the generic but reassuring conventional life may seem preferable to the risks that come from pursuing their individual callings. Similarly, some people may search for ready-made answers, trying to delegate the fundamental task of answering their most personal questions. When feeling unsure about what to pursue in life, they turn to self-help books for clear instructions and principles to live by. Alternatively, they may consult books reporting academic and statistical research on what makes people happy, with evidence-based suggestions like seeking friendship, increasing time spent in nature, and getting married. But statistics are all about averages, while there is no such thing as an average person.

These studies about what most people find fulfilling say very little about what makes each one of us feel fulfilled. We are not all called to pursue the same goal or the same life, and much would be gained if we accepted our radical differences in this respect.

It is not just the values of the majority that constitute conventionality, but also the norms dictated by all kinds of distinctive groups. These communities are formed around shared (partial) identities such as religious and spiritual beliefs, political inclinations and social causes, hobbies and professional careers, drugs of choice, and ethnic and gender identities. All these groups share a pull to merge individual personalities and unique experiences into the collective identity. Even groups that have emerged specifically to advocate for the voices of those marginalized in the dominant culture risk creating overly rigid norms of behavior for their members.

And rigid norms may leave us unprepared to deal with challenges. If we follow the trite and superficial prescriptions of the conventional life, indeed, we may soon realize that they are inadequate outside of a very narrow scope. When we experience losses and failures, the conventional life may provide little to help us cope, except suggesting denial of the negative experiences in themselves. And unaccustomed to questioning our motivations and goals, we risk missing opportunities for self-exploration and change ushered by these times of crisis and transition.

As a child, I was fascinated by the adventures of Marco Polo. Better known in Italy than in the United States, he was a Venetian merchant and an explorer of Asia along the Silk Road. Once he returned from his travels, he wrote an account of his adventures in his *Book of the Marvels of the World*, published around 1300, which detailed customs, tales, and cultures then unknown to European audiences. During his travels, he met and befriended the Mongol ruler Kublai Khan, under whose tutelage he lived for many years in Zhangjiakou, in modern-day China. Marco Polo's character made it into the illustrated books of my childhood, with his awesome adventures and insatiable curiosity. Later, I rediscovered Marco Polo in the rendition by the Italian author Italo Calvino. In his book *Invisible Cities*, Calvino imagined Marco Polo conversing with Kublai Khan about other, even more distant cities. In this account, the cities described are imaginary ones such as: a city suspended over an abyss, a city ever expanding and yet microscopic, and a city with no inhabitants. These imagined cities become places that shed new light on our culture and ourselves—the adventure this time is the search for meaning in life. "You take delight not in a city's seven or seventy wonders," says Marco Polo in *Invisible Cities*, "but in the answer it gives to a question of yours."[5] Reading Calvino as a teenager, my mind was engrossed again with Marco Polo and these new explorations.

Explorers and sailors, literary figures, astronauts and scientists, heroes of all kinds, gods and mythological figures, professional athletes, preachers and spiritual guides, CEOs and politicians—among many others—populate the fantasy lives of children and adults alike. We learn about them by reading books and watching the news, by hearing their deeds described by teachers and peers, by seeing people around us praising them or praying to them. Most often, we borrow these exalted figures from the inner worlds of our parents, for instance by internalizing the excitement our parents show whenever they talk about their favorite heroes.

These real and fictional figures stir our imagination and creativity. They help us realize what questions we care about. They make us believe, even just temporarily, that the extraordinary is reachable and that we may transcend the limits of our circumstances. Most importantly, they provide us templates for our grandiosity and callings. It does not matter that our personal deeds might not compare in magnitude with those of our heroes. With these larger-than-life figures at our side, we can better cope with difficulties and imagine our lives as purposeful.

For young children, parents themselves can be such grand figures. Toddlers swoon when they witness their parents open a glass jar with their bare hands, pick up a toy from an unreachable shelf, catch a fish at the lake, or navigate the complexities of an airport. Children, through their imagination, transform their parents into a perfect ideal: powerful, all-loving, and fully devoted adults—the first template of grandiose fantasies. Yet, over time, parents naturally lose their appeal. Tired, distracted, scared, or anxious, parents will reveal their vulnerabilities—no matter how well concealed. This process is not necessarily the result of bad parenting; it is merely due to children recognizing that their parents are people, not gods.

When the idealized parents lose their appeal, children may seek new templates for their grandiose fantasies. As a creative solution to this problem, some children may daydream that the parents they live with are not their real parents. They may fantasize about having been adopted or stolen away from their "real parents," who are of a higher status, wealth, and grandeur. This way, the imagined perfect parents still exist, just waiting to reconnect with their long-lost children. Sigmund Freud called these fantasies "family romances," romanticized stories created by children so they can elevate themselves by association with these new grandiose figures.[6] We can find many examples of these family romances in fairy tales, where young men and women born into humble circumstances are rightfully reinstated to their elevated status by either marrying royalty or discovering their true noble birth.

When our actual or imagined parents cease to be viable models for our grandiosity, we often look for other templates in the people celebrated by our society. For me, as an example, Marco Polo—the man and the fictional character—became a model of curiosity and courage to imitate.

Much can be said about a society by surveying which lives are being celebrated. Hopefully, we are presented with a diverse set of images of grandiosity to foster our psychological development. First, because of individual differences in values and personalities, we need a *variety* of templates of grandiosity, so that we can easily visualize all the possible life trajectories we might pursue. It has to be accepted that callings and well-lived lives may look very different from one another. Instead, presenting only a narrow range of narratives of success may discourage us from being creative and imaginative as we decide what to pursue in life.

The second dimension is the *depth* of the figures celebrated. A society can celebrate as heroes those who discerned their unique callings, embraced risks and sacrifices, and actively committed to their causes. These grand figures stir our fantasies in ways that are enlivening because they show strength, courage, and persistence. Our society, on the other hand, seems to focus on figures without much depth. These are the celebrities who are known not for their deeds, but because they project a cartoonish image of success, making a caricature of both calling and heroism. Many people seem to be famous based on their being famous—a circular logic—rather than for any actual achievement. In this regard, it is amazing to observe how much effort we put into following the lives of these celebrities, the ups and especially the downs: failed marriages, substance abuse issues, and career declines. We are rarely stirred by these stories and seldom express empathy for them, but rather we enjoy being distracted and numbed as we comfortably fall back on the conventional life of gossip, envy, and our own mediocrity.

While society can help us by offering viable templates for grandiosity, ultimately the responsibility to engage with our lives falls on us as individuals. If we passively retreat into the conventional life—uncritically adopting the figures celebrated by our society as molds—our lives become stunted.

The Russian author Leo Tolstoy explored the conventional life in his novella *The Death of Ivan Ilyich*, completed in 1886. Just a few years earlier, Tolstoy had struggled with a life crisis of his own, which led him to repudiate his previous writings, including the famous *War and Peace*, and seek a renewed sense of purpose. Tolstoy described Ivan Ilyich's life as an ordinary life, "ordinary and dreadful in the extreme."[7] "All the distractions of childhood and youth," those stirrings and fantasies that can enliven us, "passed him by leaving scarcely a trace; he had succumbed to both sensuality and vanity, and then in the top classes to liberal thinking, but always within limits."[8] Instead, he graduated from law school and pursued positions based on how socially respectable they were, ultimately becoming an esteemed judge, always "convinced of the need to follow the path of duty—duty being anything so designated by higher authority."[9] He moved from one city to the next, seeking higher pay and title, even if each time he had to leave behind the friendships he had tentatively started to establish. As it was proper, he courted a woman from a good family and wealth. "Ivan Ilyich had no clear and definite plans for marriage, but once the girl fell in love with him, he began to wonder—When all's said and done, why shouldn't I get married?" After all, "the match met with the approval of the society," and by marrying, "he was appealing to his superiors and their sense of propriety."[10]

His marriage, not surprisingly, was not happy. Ivan Ilyich concluded that "although married life did provide some conveniences, it was actually rather complex and difficult business."[11] Consequently, he decided that he would *perform* his role, to give his marriage "an air of harmless respectability" while guarding against disruptions to the "enjoyment and decency" of his life. He became completely absorbed in work. He played cards weekly with some acquaintances of his, while growing distant from his wife. If the novella was written today, it might only need to substitute playing cards with playing videogames.

Seeking an unproblematic and respectable life, Ivan Ilyich even achieved a level of contentment, if not mitigated happiness. It took the shock of an incurable illness, confining him to his deathbed, to wake him up to the superficiality of his relationships, to the absence of passion, love, and honesty in his life. Instead of engaging with his calling and climbing up his mountain, he had followed the conventional life. "It's as if I had gone downhill when I thought I was going uphill. That's how it was. In society's opinion I was heading uphill, but in equal measure life was slipping away from me ... And now it's all over."[12] The questions he had evaded for so long emerged anew, an opportunity to shake off his unconsciousness, to approach at least his own death with courage:

> "Maybe I didn't live as I should have done?" came the sudden thought. "But how can that be when I did everything properly?" he wondered, instantly dismissing as a total impossibility the one and only solution to the mystery of life and death.[13]

Notes

1. Jung, *Development of Personality*, 173.
2. Hillman, "The Feeling Function," 145.
3. Dante, *Inferno*, III, 36.
4. Dante, *La Divina Commedia: Inferno*, ed. Tommaso Di Salvo, 43. My translation.
5. Calvino, *Invisible Cities*, 44.
6. See Freud, "Family Romances."
7. Tolstoy, *Death of Ivan Ilyich*, 166.
8. Tolstoy, *Death of Ivan Ilyich*, 167.
9. Tolstoy, *Death of Ivan Ilyich*, 166.
10. Tolstoy, *Death of Ivan Ilyich*, 170.
11. Tolstoy, *Death of Ivan Ilyich*, 172.
12. Tolstoy, *Death of Ivan Ilyich*, 209.
13. Tolstoy, *Death of Ivan Ilyich*, 210.

References

Calvino, I. *Invisible Cities*. Orlando, Florida: Harcourt, 1974.
Dante. *La Divina Commedia: Inferno*, edited by T. Di Salvo. Bologna, Italy: Zanichelli, 1985.
Freud, S. "Family Romances." In *The Standard Edition of The Complete Psychological Works of Sigmund Freud*, edited and translated by James Strachey. Vol. 9, 235–241. New York: W. W. Norton, 1981. First published 1908.

Hillman, J. "The Feeling Function." In *Lectures on Jung's Typology*, edited by M.-L. von Franz and J. Hillman, 95–178. Putnam, Connecticut: Spring Publications, 2013.

Jung, C. G. *The Development of Personality*. Vol. 17 of *The Collected Works of C. G. Jung*, edited by H. Read, M. Fordham, G. Adler, and W. McGuire. Translated by R. F. C. Hull. Princeton, NJ: Princeton University Press, 1954.

Tolstoy, L. *The Death of Ivan Ilyich*. In *The Death of Ivan Ilyich and Other Stories*. London: Penguin, 2008.

11

WAYS TO IDENTIFY OUR GRANDIOSITY AND CALLINGS

"Am I living as I should?"—We could ponder with Tolstoy if we are living in accord with our callings. Pulled in all directions by the opinions of relatives and friends, cultural norms, and our own competing desires and interests, we may struggle to identify what to pursue—and which fantasies to leave behind. When we become overwhelmed by these decisions, we may be tempted to fall back on the conventional life and its one-size-fits-all answers to our fundamental questions. Yet, while conventional life comes with much external reinforcement, there is no guarantee it will lead us to fulfillment. The alternative is to intentionally become aware of the grandiose fantasies that animate us, trying to identify among them our unique callings, those paths that can give us a sense of purpose. Alas, it is not easy to recognize our callings.

Some people may struggle to even name their grandiose fantasies and strivings, so that discerning among them those that are worth pursuing seems the lesser problem. While family and friends may have an easier time pointing our grandiosity out for us, we may find it difficult to look dispassionately at our own motivations.

One of the reasons it is difficult to observe our grandiosity is that we may feel shame for the grandeur of our ambitions. We may have been taught to "tone down" our enthusiasm, to "grow up" and make realistic plans, and to "be humble." Culturally, these constricting messages are especially loud in the lives of women and minorities, who are often pushed into being invisible and unassuming. Because of this shame, whenever grandiose thoughts come to mind, we may push them aside, together with all the energy they bring. We may think ourselves childish or arrogant for having such fantasies—but no fantasy is arrogant or problematic in and of itself, at least until we decide to act it out. What is so wrong with imagining ourselves elected president of the country? It can be so exciting, and even humbling—do we know what we would do once in office? It is to pursue the position without being competent that is truly arrogant.

Exploring our grandiosity can also give us vertigo—at those heights, we may feel on unstable footing; toning it down and conforming may make us more comfortable. Some of our ambitions scare us when we correctly recognize that we will never be able to accomplish them, lacking the needed time, skills, experience, or talents. For instance, we may be too old to pursue these goals, or they may require greater artistic talent, mathematical abilities, patience, or physical strength than we possess. Whenever we take our fantasies too literally, we may be confronted by a sudden deflation of our self-esteem—we abruptly realize that we cannot shoot for the moon.

Daytime fantasies and nighttime dreams, however, often propose larger-than-life images as a way to awaken us to our life work and creative energy. For instance, musicians of all levels can dream of playing at Carnegie Hall; some may end up realizing such a dream, but most will only have the image as an inspiring fantasy, which continues to motivate them to practice their instruments and engage with music—a fantasy that is innocuous if they avoid taking it too concretely. Fantasies, indeed, are not the same as to-do lists; they may be there just for exploration and inspiration.

Lastly, some people may not approach their grandiose fantasies because they are concerned that their loved ones would feel hurt by such ambitions. In some relationships, love may drive one or both partners to dampen their personal dreams, their individual desires for adventure and fulfillment, lest the other person feels forgotten or secondary. I remember working with a young man who had a most ambivalent relationship with his ambitions—a desire for grandeur mixed with intense shame. We learned over time that this was an old feeling for him, having grown up with a younger brother born with a debilitating intellectual disability. To my patient, having a full and exciting life seemed like an insult to his brother's circumstances; he unconsciously had committed to a drab life. In summary, shame, fear of our imagination, and social pressure to be like everyone else can create such confusion that many people are neither in touch with their grandiosity nor virtuous; having abandoned the task of self-knowledge, they become (psychologically) lazy.

There may be times in our lives, however, when we are able to overcome these obstacles and hesitations, so we can observe our grandiosity and begin discerning our callings. Some people may be driven into these explorations by feelings of emptiness, depression, or boredom—and they may be actively looking for *something* that has energy within themselves. Other people may begin to reflect on their callings when they recognize that they are caught in between competing aspirations. For instance, they may be stuck in a moral conflict between their current ambitions and a wish to live with decency, honesty, and self-respect. Or they may be struggling because loyalties to other people conflict with their own desires. Lastly, some may start thinking about their callings when grand plans end up in failure—as it may happen to Sisyphus types—or when they realize that time is beginning to run out—a common experience for Puer types.

As we engage in these explorations, we need to remind ourselves that grandiosity and callings do not refer only to our career paths. Jobs and business endeavors being only one of the avenues to fulfillment, our callings may instead revolve around strengthening relationships, expressing our creativity, pursuing knowledge, living morally, experiencing nature, or being connected with something greater than us—or deep within. So many, especially the young, focus immediately on career changes as soon as they start to ponder about their lives' purpose, but this is undoubtedly too restrictive of an approach.

Another way in which we unduly restrict our explorations is by elevating *thinking* as the best tool for making important decisions in life, so much that "a well-thought-out choice" is taken as a synonym for "the right choice." We write down lists of pros and cons. We gather more and more information about possible options. We strive to be logical and detached in our decision-making process. We seek external, "objective" feedback from our friends and mentors. We take values inventories and personality tests. However, this approach betrays our general distrust toward other faculties that may guide us through options and to fulfillment: our intuitions and feelings.

Rather than through rational decision-making, we are more likely to identify our grandiose fantasies by stumbling upon them, for instance when we are lost in daydreaming—on our commute, showering, talking in therapy without a set agenda, or walking in nature. After all, we do not create a calling, and surely not by thinking about it. On the contrary, a calling is the condition of being acted upon, of being moved by something seemingly outside of ourselves, be it a passion, an obsession, a fantasy, or a vision.

Whether it is discovering rock climbing as a favorite hobby, becoming passionate about a social cause, having a business idea, engaging with the unconscious, or feeling touched by a yoga retreat, grandiosity and callings grab our attention by stirring us. Intuitions arriving with such force cannot be forgotten: we do not need to write them down to remember them. Instead, they keep us awake at night or make us giggle out loud—in many ways, we seem possessed by them.

Grandiosity and callings can stir us to such degree, that they arguably resemble the experience of being in love. Like our callings, romantic love resists our will and defies logic. We cannot force ourselves into loving somebody. A choice of a partner based on logic, reason, and social propriety does not make love appear. In our times of instantaneous gratification, dating apps, and matches generated by computer algorithms, love remains a spontaneous and elusive experience we cannot control. In the English language, love is described as something that happens *to* us: we say falling in love, struck by love, head over heels, infatuated, lovesick, and being crazy about someone. But we cannot say, for instance, I made myself love him. The truth is that at most we can be open to the experience when it presents itself. And love retains its agency to leave, in which case we say, just as passively, that we fell out of love.

It is not only that grandiose fantasies stir us like romantic love does, but also that our experiences of love can be expressions of grandiosity. When we love someone, we elevate their status; their beauty, qualities, and virtues are exalted. Each of their gestures and words is perceived as if infused with deeper meaning. Ordinary and mundane activities done with our beloveds—grocery shopping, driving to work—carry intense energy. When artists depict their beloveds, and when they show up in our dreams, they appear as special, unique, more than mere mortals.

The exaltation of romantic love also affects our self-esteem and potential for creativity. When our love is reciprocated, we become confident, elated, and energetic. Through conversations with our beloveds, we rediscover long-lost passions and dreams, and we share secrets and past hurts that were holding us back. We find courage we did not expect to have, and not just for the courtship or often, falling in love initiates personal life changes, like career transitions or overcoming a period of grief after a loss. The end of love can be just as transformative; a breakup or a divorce, in addition to bringing on mourning, can be a crisis that pushes us to explore our own motivations and needs, and to identify new ways of relating to others.

Because it brings us to such extremes—elation and dejection, idealization of the other and of ourselves, crises and dramatic life changes—we can recognize that romantic love itself is a calling. The psychoanalyst Ethel Person wrote:

> Love creates a situation in which the [ego] is exposed to new risks and enlarged possibilities; it is one of the most significant crucibles for growth. Romantic love takes on meaning and provides a subjective sense of liberation only insofar as it creates a flexibility in personality that allows a break-through of internal psychological barriers and taboos, and sometimes external ones as well. It creates a flux in personality, the possibility for change, and the impetus to begin new phases of life and undertake new endeavors. As such, it can be seen as a paradigm for any significant realignment of personality and values; in this way it resembles the great religious conversion experiences.[1]

But no lover, book, teacher, therapist, or test can identify for us our own grandiose fantasies; it would be harder still for them to identify which, among those, are callings personally worth pursuing. To find our own answers, we have to engage in personal explorations and gather data about ourselves. In addition to paying attention to our emotions and enthusiasms, I discuss other possible ways to become conscious of our grandiosity and callings, such as journaling, introspection, psychotherapy, nighttime dreams, and meaningful experiences outside of our comfort zone.

Journaling is available to all, anytime we seek greater insight into ourselves. Instead of mindlessly jumping from one thought to the next, we can take time to write them all down in a free-flowing form, together with any accompanying feelings. Rereading them later, we can try to notice the recurring questions we ask ourselves, the fantasies that stir us, and the self-talk we engage in. This is not an easy task, because the thoughts that run through our mind are like mental background-noise that we do not even detect anymore. The written page becomes a mirror to notice these thoughts as if we are hearing them from the outside in, gaining some degree of objectivity.

By introspection, I mean taking some time to reflect on our motivations and goals. Usually, we mindlessly involve ourselves in endeavors that end up taking over our lives. Then, we quickly and breathlessly move from task to task, caught in Sisyphean work. Engrossed in our grandiose pursuits, we may struggle to pause long enough to realize that there are other fantasies competing for our attention. Alternatively, we can decide to slow down and explore our fantasies before pursuing them—there has to be some quiet time for reflection in our hectic lives.

As an example, I share the story of a man in his mid-thirties who, after a decade spent doggedly and brilliantly working to grow his start-up, finally sold it for a small fortune. Unsure about what to do next, he immediately began to look for a new venture. In doing so, he felt compelled to replicate the excitement, challenges, and achievements he had experienced building his first start-up. He felt such pressure, that he found himself in a panicky frenzy. In therapy, I learned that he often thought of a quote—supposedly an old Chinese proverb—that has been making its rounds online, "The best time to plant a tree was twenty years ago. The second-best time is now." He interpreted the proverb as suggesting that he had to start another company, and quickly.

Apart from all this pressure to repeat his business escapades, he happened to be a delightful and caring man. Father of two toddlers, his face would light up when he talked about his children. At that time, being in transition and not working most days, he spent much time playing with them in all kinds of creative ways. Unique among the men I have met, he was happy when the babysitter was sick, as it gave him an excuse to spend his whole day with his children.

Listening to his stories, I wondered how we figure out which specific trees we should attend to. Rather than imposing arbitrary goals on ourselves, we may benefit from simply observing which activities we already happen to enjoy the most; for instance, those interests we are drawn to whenever we have free time. Enjoyment, indeed, can be a way to identify our callings. In this man's case, his entrepreneurial past had given him much to be proud of. But people's sources of energy and satisfaction can, and usually do, change over the course of their lives. It seemed to me that for him, fatherhood was a tree already planted—ripe with fruits and enjoyment—which he had long ignored when he ran his business and was hardly home. He had achieved his professional goals, he had brought the stone to the peak, and now there was an opportunity for change. But, caught by ongoing grandiose dreams of financial and professional successes, he could not slow down and think differently about this new phase of his life. He could not ponder the "crazy idea" of choosing family over work, even just for a few years, a choice that would have forced him to revisit his idea of masculinity and success.

If we want to be deliberate in discerning our callings, we can start by asking questions about the grandiose fantasies that are tempting us. Is this an old dream of mine or a new emerging one? What would my daily life look like if I started working toward such a goal? What do I hope to accomplish? Am I seeking external validation, or following an inner sense of purpose? What sacrifices might this grandiose endeavor entail? What sacrifices would I be willing to bear? How might those around me be affected by my efforts? How do I anticipate I will feel once I accomplish this goal? What other pursuits would I have to give up to chase this one? Is this a fantasy that is best left unlived, or do I actually want to undertake it?

The therapeutic encounter has the potential of bringing new insight into our grandiose fantasies, too. In therapy, we can become more familiar with the inner questions that shape our lives and cultivate awareness of our motivations. The therapist and the patient together create a space that is quite radical, because it defies the ego-driven pressure for speediness, productivity, and multitasking that permeates so many of our interactions. Two people commit to sit without distractions and talk about what they sense as important—without checking their phones, for one hour! And in contrast with the constraints—real or perceived—of the conventional life, in therapy we are invited to freely speak our mind, without needing to impress, perform, or conform—this being an invitation that is often difficult to embrace, so unaccustomed are we to spontaneity.

Over time and through empathy, the therapist functions as a mirror, highlighting those qualities, virtues, and aspirations that were initially hidden away. But far from being self-indulgent, the conversations are often challenging, because the therapist can also point out those rote approaches to life that are holding us back, tying us to our Puer fantasies or Sisyphean strivings even when life may be calling us in different directions. By encouraging an honest exploration of our emotions, intuitions, motivations, narratives, and the unconscious, therapy opens us up to otherness within—the space where callings emerge. And the contributions of the therapist, which are rooted in the therapist's personality and worldview, further introduce otherness and multiple perspectives into our explorations. When it pushes us outside of our comfort zone, therapy has the effect of relativizing the ego, as if the mirror of the Snow White fairy tale were to say, "My queen, you may be the fairest in your small world, but truly there are other meaningful approaches to life, and you may benefit from considering them."

Because our grandiosity presents as larger-than-life expressions of ambition, purpose, power, drive, arrogance, excitement, or selflessness, it would be easy for the therapist to interpret and decode each of these as dangerous, exhibitionistic, narcissistic, or immoral—implying that grandiosity always has to be renounced as a childish, inappropriate desire. By not embracing the complexities of the grandiose fantasies, the therapist would end up enforcing some idea of normalcy and so unwittingly reinforce what conventionality already loudly says. As Donald Winnicott wrote, psychotherapy can instead help us achieve "some measure of insanity," a freedom to be spontaneous and creative: these being assets that can free us all from the deadening effects of the conventional life.[2]

It has actually been my experience that patients caught in destructive or meaningless-to-them grandiose pursuits can only heal by exploring other, new grandiose pursuits. In fact, they may find it impossible to simply disengage and let their current compulsions of habit go. By exploring the totality of their grandiose fantasies in therapy, they may be able to identify new callings—just as energetic as their current compulsions—that can reorient their conscious efforts and provide them with new viewpoints on life and new sources of satisfaction and meaning.

Another way to explore our callings is our nighttime dreams. Dream interpretation was central to the psychoanalytic approaches initially developed by Sigmund Freud, Carl Jung, and others at the turn of the twentieth century. Because dreams are a truly spontaneous creation from within, Freud called them the royal road to the unconscious, allowing unfiltered access to our underlying wishes and fears. By contrast, journaling, therapy, and other forms of introspection are more strongly colored by whom we think we *should* be and how we want to be perceived by others. Over the decades, however, psychological theories have moved away from focusing on the unconscious, and even further away from dream interpretation—Jungian psychology being a notable exception to the trend. This shift was most accentuated in the United States (as compared to Europe), where psychology as a formal discipline has aimed to be seen as a science, like medicine, and so has adopted the methods and language of the sciences. The practice of psychotherapy has similarly gravitated toward secular, no-nonsense, and pragmatic approaches. Dream interpretation—with its inevitable ambiguity and subjectivity—poorly fits within these trends.

Dreams resist rational thinking and linear explanation; instead, they evoke confusing feelings, symbols, and wishes from the depths of our personality. Unsure about what to do with these experiences, we risk dismissing them as curious yet irrelevant. In fact, it is exactly when we are unfamiliar with our inner world of fantasies that dreams are most helpful, bringing into view aspects of ourselves we may have never thought about before.

In my life, I found much needed validation in a dream when, in my mid-twenties, I contemplated leaving my academic pursuits in economics. Thanks to the emotional experiences in home hospice and the introspection that I so sorely needed at the time, including through therapy, I explored more honestly my motivations and goals. And ultimately, I realized that engaging with questions related to meaning and callings was a true passion of mine. I wondered whether I could do work similar to my volunteering experiences in home hospice, while also making an income. Over time, the idea of retraining as a psychologist started to take shape.

Steeped in Jungian psychology, I started paying attention to my nighttime dreams; I did not want to make any changes by ego alone. To that end, I kept a notebook at my bedside and wrote down my dreams whenever I could remember them. It was at that time that I dreamt the following:

> Even if the pope is still in office, I am elected pope too, with his approval. I have to speak to the believers but also to the unbelievers. I am frightened by the grandness of the role, but in any case, I can say that, because all popes say the ritual sentence: "I am not worthy of this role."

Being elected pope, talk about grandiosity! I knew, however, that I did not want to become a priest—or a pope. After all, I did not grow up religious and, back then, I did not identify with any organized faith. Such is the language of the unconscious and dreams: often bombastic, always symbolic, and capable of stirring our emotions and imagination. For me personally, being elected pope meant to become a guide, an intermediary who could help others relate the daily, prosaic aspects of their lives to their search for meaning and purpose.

The sentence mentioned in the dream—"I am not worthy of this role"—turned out to be more than just the fruit of my imagination. After having the dream, I learned that the Catholic Church had a similar ritual following the election of a new pope. From the fifteenth to the twentieth century, as part of a new pope's coronation ceremony in St. Peter's Basilica, the ceremonial procession would stop three times. Each time, a bundle of flax attached to a gilded staff was burned to ashes before the new pope, and a master of ceremonies would proclaim, *Pater Sancte sic transit gloria mundi*—"Holy Father, so passes worldly glory!" This was meant as a reminder of mortality and the impermanence of all earthly achievements, an aide for the pope to avoid self-aggrandizing fantasies. Similar to this tradition, my dream contained a "ritual sentence" to rebalance its grandiose energy, a call to modesty as I jumped forward into a new career.

This dream strengthened my resolve to pursue a second doctorate and become a psychologist. Career changes—with their fantasies of new beginnings and second chances—are grandiose undertakings. It was reassuring to find out that two psychotherapists I know, the first a mentor of mine and the other a patient, to find out that had similar dreams of becoming priests when they considered pursuing a career in our field. Like me, they interpreted their dreams as callings, affirming their desire to work with patients seeking more lasting fulfillment and sense of purpose.

Lastly, experiences outside of our comfort zone have the potential of waking us up, pushing us to reassess how we are living and what we are pursuing. First among these experiences, as terrible as they are, are any brushes with death—of our loved ones or ours. As a thought exercise, I sometimes ask patients to imagine themselves old and looking back at their own lives. Of all our accomplishments, which ones would still be worth a mention on our deathbed? Which ones would strike us as futile or vain? Of all our disappointments and failures, which ones will ultimately seem like small detours from the overall trajectory of our lives? Which of our passions and fantasies will we regret pursuing? And which will we regret *not* pursuing? It would be sad to wait until it is too late to engage with our callings, as Ivan Ilyich did in Tolstoy's novella. Instead, we can light a little imaginary fire under ourselves, move outside of our comfort zone—also with thoughts of mortality—and start exploring what really matters to us, what is calling for us.

Notes

1. I have substituted her word "self" with "ego," for ease of understanding. Person, *Dreams of Love*, xxiii.
2. Winnicott, vol. 7 of *The Collected Works*, 116. A book on the two-sidedness of every narrative, including the fluid distinction between wisdom and insanity, is Guggenbühl-Craig, *Old Fool*.

References

Guggenbühl-Craig, A. *The Old Fool and the Corruption of Myth*. Putnam, Connecticut: Spring Publications, 1991.
Person, E. S. *Dreams of Love and Fateful Encounters: The Power of Romantic Passion*. Washington, DC: American Psychiatric Publishing, 2007.
Winnicott, D. W. Vol. 7 of *The Collected Works of D. W. Winnicott*. edited by L. Caldwell, H.T. Robinson, R. Adès and A. T. Kabesh. Oxford: Oxford University Press, 2017.

PART IV

The courage of our insignificance

12

THE COURAGE TO ABSTAIN

Muffler Installation Dealers' Associated Service, better known as Midas Muffler, was founded in the 1950s and quickly became a successful franchise of car repair shops in the United States. The founder's grandson, Jeremy Sherman, received an initial share of his inheritance when he was only 16 years old. This wealth, however, filled him with a lifelong supply of guilt. For years, he asked himself nagging questions about his value as a person. He felt compelled to live a life that showed him worthy of his financial status. Like the Greek myth of King Midas, wealth came with a problematic, shadow side.[1]

As a young man, Sherman resolved to pursue virtue. He dropped out of college and joined a rural commune, relinquishing his personal possessions to take the required vow of poverty. There, he engaged in hard manual labor, including farming, and got married. After six years of communal life, however, he started feeling unsettled. Unsure if living away from society was as meaningful as he initially thought, he left the commune and his pursuit of an ascetic life. When he inherited an even larger portion of his family's wealth, he decided he would find a way to use it for the greater good. Inspired by a lecture on the nuclear arms race, he co-founded a grassroots lobbying campaign for nuclear disarmament. He also threw himself into supporting global environmental initiatives. Deeming these as worthy causes, Sherman hoped he had aligned his life trajectory with his callings.

Yet again he found himself unsettled. With his fortieth birthday approaching, he was moved to introspection, realizing he was neither content nor feeling he had much to show for all his efforts. He admitted to himself that social activism was not his passion; it was something he thought he *should* do, given his wealth and liberal values. And his crisis of meaning was worsened by his divorce and the death of both his parents. It was at that time that Sherman reflected back on something his father used to say, about the need to embrace the "courage of one's insignificance." His father had struggled with similar conflicts related to wealth, familial responsibilities, and personal interests. In fact, Sherman's father was an artistic man, engaged in both the cultural life and social unrest of the 1960s, but who ultimately decided to go the corporate route and run the Midas Muffler family business.

Thinking about his father's advice, Jeremy Sherman began exploring some of the questions he had been avoiding all along—tackling those conflicts possibly inherited from his father together with the family wealth. Explorations about our own motivations—so uniquely personal—have the power of radically changing the direction of our lives. Sherman finally became aware of how guilt, and not callings, had driven his life choices. He realized that he was grandiosely trying to justify his affluence with virtuous life choices—as if inherited wealth happens for a reason, rather than merely due to the lottery of life. Once he gave up these impossible fantasies, he suddenly ceased feeling so exceptional, wounded, and wanting—he felt more at peace with his life circumstances. Free to focus on his own interests without having to justify them, Sherman went back to graduate school and has since remained engaged in intellectual and philosophical work, finally feeling engrossed in his endeavors. He has published a book for a prestigious university press, exploring biological and philosophical questions related to life's purpose. While I might not subscribe to his preferred philosophy, I surely wish him well in his personal search for meaning.

Courage—of letting go of some of our grandiose fantasies, while embracing those that are our callings—and insignificance—the acceptance of our limitations and lot in life—frame the discussion in these concluding chapters. We are all pulled in many directions by our fantasies of knowledge, money, virtue, fame, and youth, to name a few. If we disavow all grandiosity within, then we are left with little energy, passion, or creativity—we fall back on the conventional life. If instead we become aware of what stirs us, we find ourselves at a crossroads of competing fantasies and strivings. There, we need to pause for a moment and look down each road as far as we can, wondering where each endeavor would lead us. Some of these paths may be callings worth pursuing, but others—like those discussed in the rest of this chapter—are best left behind, even if they seem superficially compelling.

One reason to abstain from a grandiose endeavor is the realization that it comes with unacceptable costs. We already discussed how grandiose pursuits always entail sacrifices for those chasing them, as well as their families, friends, and communities. To consciously choose which strivings are worth the costs, then, we have to become aware of what is at stake. I once worked with a young man, a physician in training, who was pursuing his professional life with great vigor. He was involved in clinical training, research projects, hospital committees, additional volunteering efforts, and even health-related business ventures. His life was full of energy and movement, and his professional trajectory was on the rise. However, rather than being content, he was painfully anxious. To me, he seemed incredibly competitive, to the point of being abrasive and dismissive. He had the following dream:

> We are all rock climbing up a rather vertical wall. It is part of a competition and there is only one winner: the one who arrives first. I am doing a great job at it, and for a while I do not even see those around me, leaping up and up. Suddenly, I see my classmate Elisa climbing next to me—and without thinking, I push her. I see her falling down toward the rocky ground. I wake up horrified by what I did.

Of note, he had never rock climbed in his life; echoing the myth of Sisyphus, climbing often appears in dreams as a symbol of our grandiose ambitions. To understand what this dream might be suggesting, I invited my patient to explore the image of him pushing Elisa off the cliff.

Jung suggested that there are two ways to interpret dreams.[2] The interpretation at the "objective" level takes the dream as a commentary on the *external* situation and relationships of the dreamer. When we dream of a friend, for instance, we may interpret the dream as highlighting or uncovering our feelings toward that specific person. In this light, the dream previously discussed would be seen as a commentary on my patient's relationship with Elisa, his peer. But we quickly assessed that he did not harbor hostile feelings toward her. They were specializing in different areas of medicine, not directly competing for accolades or positions. My patient was actually quite fond of her as a colleague and enjoyed interacting with her whenever the occasion presented itself.

The interpretation of a dream at the "subjective" level, instead, "refers every part of the dream and all the actors in it back to the dreamer."[3] From this perspective, then, we would think of Elisa as part of the *inner* life of my patient—a symbol for a side of his personality. I asked more about her—whom he had never mentioned before in therapy—and anything that would come to mind when thinking of her. He enjoyed her company, he shared, because "Elisa is our nicest classmate. She is always in a good mood and so caring, asking everyone how they are doing in school and in their lives. She is such a warm person." We came to consider Elisa as a symbol of his own caring and warm side, hence understanding the dream in its entirety as a commentary on his grandiosity and its costs.

His desire to climb to the top and "win in life" was shown to result in the sacrifice of the caring and relational side of his personality—an interpretation that had a visible emotional impact on him. It was his cutthroat approach, the exclusive focus on career advancement, that made him feel unsettled in the dream and beyond. Hence, his dream could be seen as an invitation to reexamine his goals, as well as the ways in which he was pursuing them—a call to abstain or at least slow down for a while, until he gained more clarity about himself. Like this young man, we too may realize that our grandiose pursuits, left unchecked, involve excessive costs, at times even pushing us to renounce our humanity, decency, and concern for both other people and ourselves.

At the crossroads of competing pursuits, we may recognize that a grandiose fantasy harks back to our past and especially to our childhood. Here too we need to abstain, looking instead for ways to move forward in life. To be clear, I am not suggesting that there is no value in looking back at our past experiences and relationships, including the formative years of childhood. These explorations into our histories help us better understand how we came to adopt our worldviews, what motivates us, and how we accommodate (or not) otherness and our limitations—the great challenges of the ego. By revisiting the past with self-compassion and curiosity, we can actually free ourselves from ineffective ways of relating to people and of attending to our needs. Furthermore, symbols related to the past and childhood—including images of auspicious childbirths, playful children, and pleasant childhood memories—may emerge spontaneously from the unconscious, especially at times of life transitions, showing up in reveries and nighttime dreams. These images evoke the figure of the *Puer Aeternus*, bring us childlike energy, enthusiasm, and exuberance. They are the expansive fantasies that open us up to new beginnings.[4]

However, it would be a mistake to pursue these backward-looking fantasies too literally. As we discussed, some people may aim at the actual restoration of their youthfulness, whether through plastic surgery or by dating a much younger partner. Others may seek to always start anew, by routinely changing cities, friends, spouses, jobs, careers, or religions. By leaving their histories behind, they impossibly hope to undo them. Still others may give up their adult lives and decide to return to their childhood towns and homes—a decision that may not be heartfelt, but instead driven by a nostalgic wish for a do-over. For all, this is a return to the psychology of the Puer, to a time when we were naive, untouched by failure, unaware of our own limitations, and not committed to any path. Rather than simply remembering, we try to recreate the past: these fantasies signal a refusal to accept the inexorable march of time.

An Italian woman in her early thirties came to therapy shortly after a breakup. Having immigrated to Chicago to live with her boyfriend, she was now overwhelmed trying to decide what to do next. She was hurt by how the relationship had unfolded, feeling confused about her share of responsibility for the many arguments and misunderstandings. With some hesitation, she shared that she was unsure about therapy, wondering how talking was going to help her. She often thought about simply returning to Italy and starting anew there. A few weeks into therapy, she had the following dream:

> I am driving back home. But instead of my parents' actual home—they always lived in a condo in the center of the city—it is a big villa surrounded by beautiful gardens with trees and flowers of every kind. Following the road, and as I get closer to this villa, I notice that the gate to the property is shut. On the road, big rocks block any access. I then see a snake on these rocks, and it starts moving toward me, its mouth wide open.

The Garden of Eden. On the right, an angel preventing all from reentering. (Illustration from *The Very Rich Hours of the Duke of Berry*, 1416.)

Yet another dream that left the dreamer scared. We came to understand it as a manifestation of her grandiose fantasy of returning to childhood. Rather than moving forward in her explorations, deepening her understanding of how she approaches relationships and decisions, she seemed tempted to retreat to the familiar and comforting—her parent's home. In the imagery of the dream, their condo had been transformed into the Garden of Eden, a symbol for the blissful state of childhood and the absence of responsibilities. However, as she tried to drive back to that place, she was confronted by rocks and a snake, all but frustrating her wishes to go back in time. We ultimately saw the dream as a strong invitation—a calling—to keep developing.

In the Biblical story of the expulsion from the Garden of Eden, the snake was a catalyst for transformation. Humans moved from a place of naive bliss, where everything was provided to them, to the hard realities of life as we know it—having to work, suffer, and grow old. Psychologically, this is the movement from childhood to adulthood, and from unconsciousness to taking responsibility for our lives—a process that is indeed hard work. In the Biblical narrative, after the expulsion, the gate of the Garden was forever shut—an image that reappeared in my patient's dream—an angel guarding the entrance with a sword, preventing all from reentering. Myth and dream both point to the impossibility of moving back into our usual comfort zone—the ego trying to preserve itself unchanged—while life pushes us into new territories, giving us opportunities for psychological growth.

Just as unfulfilling are those grandiose fantasies that center on other people—*our* fantasies of what they should accomplish and who they should become. For instance, we may hope that our partners, children, or friends change in exactly the ways we think they should—"for their own good!"—often irrespective of their own wishes. Unwittingly, we create a confusing short circuit of personal responsibilities and choices. As we boost our own self-image, thinking ourselves altruistic, we miss that our motivations may be the narcissistic desire to create our ideal partners, perfect children, and forever-grateful friends. On occasion, of course, we may end up being instrumental in the genuine healing and growth of others. However, to make it our mission to change another person is most likely a distraction from our own callings—endeavors requiring personal sacrifices and transformations, not vicarious living through other people's achievements.

The fantasy of changing others is especially tempting for psychotherapists. Whether relying on Jungian or other psychoanalytic approaches, cognitive techniques, or emotion-regulation skills, to name a few, we psychotherapists naturally become eager to offer what we consider helpful, often because it has resonated deeply with us and has helped in our own lives. However, we run the risk of becoming too personally invested in proving the validity and superiority of our therapeutic approaches, seeking confirmation for them in the work with our patients, while dismissing any criticism and our own doubts.[5] We may offer to all what has worked for some, pushing our patients toward the sought-after outcome, be that a spiritual attitude, a specific way of relating, a pragmatic stance toward problems, or the abatement of intense feelings. But given the variety of minds, using Petrarch's phrase, it is grandiose to think that any one therapeutic approach will prove relevant for all. As Jung wrote, "psychotherapy has taught us that in the final reckoning it is not knowledge, not technical skill, that has a curative effect, but the personality of the doctor."[6] To this, I would add that not all personalities are a good match for one another and that there are times when we cannot help some patients despite our skills and best intentions—a humbling reminder of our limitations as psychotherapists.

Lastly, any grandiose fantasy aiming at an impossible goal is better left behind. While sometimes our grandiosity can help us see possibilities where others see none, if we recognize that an endeavor is preposterous and doomed to fail, then we show courage by abstaining from it, not by remaining on the sinking ship. And when we do not stubbornly hold onto these empty fantasies, then we free energy for other, more meaningful pursuits in our lives.

Raised by distant, unengaged parents, an American woman experienced a long series of disheartening romantic relationships. Each time, she had fallen in love with superficially charming men, who had neither her intellectual depth nor the capacity for sustained empathy. In her therapy work, she came to realize that her strongest motivation was the search for an ideal, loving partner, somebody who would finally be a balsam for her early disappointments, the wounds of childhood she carried within. Her longing for such a corrective experience was so strong that each time she met a man who showed interest in her, she unconsciously ignored all red flags. It was not that she could not rationally see the lack of potential and the shadow areas in their connection, but the fantasy of the perfect love overrode any such concerns.

At the time we started working together, she was struggling to divorce her French husband. In their relationship, he had quickly revealed a paucity of character underneath his charming exterior. He was not an equal partner, unwilling to compromise or even just converse about their plans and life together. Not only did he not share her interests and values, but he bullyingly belittled them. Within two years of marriage, he had already shifted his attention to the next shining thing: he had started an affair without any sign of regret. Upset about the idea of having to end yet another relationship, my patient had the following revelatory dream, worth sharing in its entirety:

> I am out on a boat off the coast of France. My husband is actually a fisherman: a really poor, unlucky, unattractive one. He pulls his fishing nets on the boat, and all he caught were broken shoes, empty cans, and a dead fish. This is very dismal, and I want to leave.
>
> When we arrive back at the harbor, in this little charming coastal town, I am leaving him for good. Yet, as soon as I step off the boat, a strong energy takes hold of me. I know that if I turn back and look at him, I will see him again as handsome and charming—like I saw him when I first met him—and I will be in love again. It is really hard not to turn, but I manage to just keep walking straight.

As I walk toward the main square, I see a person carrying a wheelbarrow full of masks—all with my husband's semblances. I then realize that I am in a theater set. All the houses are actually just façades propped up with scaffolding: the whole thing is fake! I am glad I did not turn back.

There is an abrupt change of scenery. I am now out in the countryside, and an old woman shows me a path carved in the rock that leads to some ancient ruins. I decide to go explore them.

In the dream, her husband brought into the relationship things with no potential: dead fish and trash. She became aware of this dismal reality and wanted to leave him. However, she was tempted again, as her grandiose fantasy about love took hold of her. She could fall in love with him anew, as if she had learned nothing about him; this way, she would once again project her hopes onto an unsuitable man. This time, however, she decided to abstain from her compulsion to love.

Her renunciation made new insights possible. She could now see clearly the truth about her pursuit of charm and romanticism; these are just appearances, masks without substance that are not going to stand the test of time. In a relationship, forced romanticism often signals powerful grandiose reinterpretations of the actual depth of the connection. Charm alone does not make a partner engaged or a relationship fulfilling. Rather than repeating her usual pattern, she gave up the impossible task of creating a love story where there was none. The last scene of the dream is the most hopeful. When the charade of the cycle was lifted, new explorations became possible. And new paths and callings become available to us all, as soon as we let go of unfeasible endeavors.

In this chapter, I discussed the case for abstaining from some kinds of grandiose pursuits. However, we cannot default to inaction. Inaction is especially tempting for Puer types, who would rather keep all options open. They risk getting caught in endless introspection, ongoing psychotherapy, always "deeper" explorations of their motivations and callings. Procrastination and indecisiveness emerge, grandiose attempts to stop the passing of time. Stuck at the crossroads of competing fantasies, Puer types may never commit to a path and see where it leads. "Just take the next bit of earth you can find," Marie-Louise von Franz urged Puer types, "plow it and plant something in it. No matter whether it is business, or teaching, or anything else, give yourself for once to that field which is ahead of you."[7] As we explore further in the next chapter, when confronted by our callings, we all ultimately need to respond with action—we need to engage.

Notes

1. Sherman, "Freeing Up," 36–8.
2. See Jung, *Psychology of the Unconscious*, par 121*ff.*
3. Jung, *Psychology of the Unconscious*, par 130*ff.*
4. See Jacoby, *Longing for Paradise*.

5. Jungian analyst Adolf Guggenbühl-Craig discussed the risks of unchecked power dynamics in the helping professions, like psychotherapy and social worker, and his insights may well apply also to social activism. Guggenbühl-Craig argued that we psychotherapists may project on our patients our own woundedness, leaving us unconscious of our hurt, doubts, and need for healing. As a corrective to such inflation, he discussed the importance for psychotherapists of receiving honest feedback from friends. He also explored the image of the "wounded healer," a therapist who "is capable of experiencing sickness as an existential possibility in himself, and of integrating it." Guggenbühl-Craig, *Power in the Helping Professions*, 98.
6. Jung, *The Development of Personality*, 140.
7. von Franz, *Puer Aeternus*, 153.

References

Guggenbühl-Craig, A. *Power in the Helping Professions*. Dallas, Texas: Spring Publications, 1971.

Jacoby, M. *Longing for Paradise: Psychological Perspectives on an Archetype*. Toronto: Inner City Books, 2006.

Jung, C. G. *The Development of Personality*. Vol. 17 of *The Collected Works of C. G. Jung*, edited by H. Read, M. Fordham, G. Adler, and W. McGuire. Translated by R. F. C. Hull. Princeton, NJ: Princeton University Press, 1954.

Jung, C. G. *On the Psychology of the Unconscious*. In *Two Essays in Analytical Psychology*. Vol. 7 of *The Collected Works of C. G. Jung*, edited by H. Read, M. Fordham, G. Adler, and W. McGuire. Translated by R. F. C. Hull. 2nd ed. Princeton, NJ: Princeton University Press, 1972.

Sherman, J. "Freeing Up." *Psychology Today*, January/February 2017.

von Franz, M.-L. *The Problem of the Puer Aeternus*. Toronto: Inner City Books, 2000.

13

THE COURAGE TO ENGAGE

If we are not aware of our motivations, we can easily slide into unfulfilling paths: the conventional life with its false promises of mass-produced happiness or our own ego-driven and narcissistic pursuits. But if we instead decide to engage with our callings—the grandiose endeavors that give our lives a sense of meaning and purpose—we find ourselves on uncharted paths. And because they inevitably require sacrifices on our part, to engage with our callings takes courage—it is always heroic.

When writing of heroism, I am not referring to those who purposely seek to be recognized as heroes. Those people pursue dangerous and physically challenging deeds, intentionally putting their lives at risk. For instance, they may choose to climb Mount Everest, travel as journalists to treacherous places, donate a kidney, or join a war. They seek these feats not because they are motivated by personal callings—as their fellow climbers, organ donors, or soldiers may be—but by the desire for a spot in the limelight. For these people, accomplishing something, anything that could be considered heroic, is in itself the goal.

But heroism is more than just impressive accomplishments and public shows of strength. Across cultures, the essence of heroism is the manifestation of one's character in the face of adversity, for instance through genuine expressions of integrity and nobility. More than the deed itself, it is for these intrinsic qualities that heroes are considered worthy of admiration. And in this sense, heroism also belongs to the lives of ordinary people who are called to deal with apparently impossible situations and who step up to meet these challenges. They do not seek danger on purpose, nor do they look around for the opportunity to shine as saviors and rescuers. But when they find themselves called to action, they engage by noticing, showing up, taking a stance, and intervening.

"Until Flight 1549, I had assumed that I would always live a pretty anonymous life," wrote Captain Chesley "Sully" Sullenberger.[1] Things changed on January 15,

2009, when a flock of geese struck his airplane seconds after takeoff, causing both engines to lose all thrust. This was an unlikely event, as nowadays pilots may go an entire career never experiencing the loss of even one engine—losing both is unheard of. Realizing what had happened, Sullenberger's first reaction was of protest against the cards he had been dealt—"This can't be happening. This doesn't happen to me."[2] Aware of the need to focus, he pushed aside distracting thoughts and became completely absorbed by the problem at hand. Together with his copilot, he continued to fly the damaged aircraft, communicated with ground control and cabin crew, and ran through emergency procedures and checklists. Unable to reach any nearby airport, he landed in the Hudson River—surrounded by New York City's skyscrapers—a mere three-and-a-half minutes after colliding with the birds. While being rescued by nearby ferries, Sullenberger's main concern was for the 154 people aboard. He shared that when he heard nobody had died, a huge burden was lifted off his heart, as if he himself had been carrying the weight of the whole universe.[3] At that moment, he felt he had become one with those he led to safety.

Many other people find themselves in similarly extraordinary situations and act just as heroically. For instance, they jump in stormy waters to rescue someone in danger. They run toward a car on fire to extricate its passengers. Or they carry a fellow wounded soldier to safety, risking death by enemy fire. For them, as it was for Sullenberger, heroism is not the sought-after goal, but a noble response to a major challenge. In the intensity of the moment, these heroes lose track of their instinct of self-preservation; their own identities grandiosely expand to include other people and even ideals considered worth dying for.

The way people respond to extreme challenges is a reflection of their character. While most of us will thankfully not face these life-or-death situations in our lives, these stories show us the importance of cultivating our character and attending to its development. Then, even our ordinary successes and failures become opportunities to strengthen our self-confidence, empathy, and courage. And by engaging with our callings, we practice responding with integrity and awareness to challenges, including those most unlikely and extreme. Actually, all of our lives are touched by life-or-death situations, for instance when we experience the death of our loved ones and approach our own, bringing us back to that final calling explored by Leo Tolstoy in *The Death of Ivan Ilyich*.

In and of itself, attending to the development of our character is a calling. Sullenberger, for instance, had prepared for the possibility of an airplane failure throughout his professional life. He witnessed the death of fellow fighter pilots due to accidents, and he had several close calls himself. During his lengthy tenure as a commercial pilot, he had been asked to investigate airplane accidents, a task that brought him to the sites of several crashes. Sullenberger's aim had always been to learn from the life-saving intuitions and tragic mistakes of other pilots, as well as his own. He was moved by a desire to contribute to the overall wisdom of his profession and to use this knowledge in developing safety trainings for generations of pilots to come. He even shared new aviation safety procedures, like the use of checklists, with other industries as a safety consultant. In his autobiography

Highest Duty: My Search for What Really Matters he related his ongoing commitment to safety also to the experience of losing his father to suicide. "Quite frankly, one of the reasons I think I've placed such a high value on life is that my father took his. ... I exercise more care in my professional responsibilities. I am willing to work very hard to protect people's lives, to be a good Samaritan, and to not be a bystander, in part because I couldn't save my father."[4]

What makes Sullenberger's deed truly heroic is his dedication to aviation and the integrity with which he performed his duties until that momentous day—how intentionally he cultivated his character and lived out his values. "One way of looking at this might be that, for 42 years, I've been making small regular deposits in this bank of education, training, and experience," he wrote, "and on January 15, the balance was sufficient so that I could make a sudden large withdrawal."[5] Too many times, unfortunately, narratives about heroism are too shallow and simplistic, focusing only on the heroic deed in itself, the single act of courage. These narratives overlook how heroes had committed to their callings long before the fateful situations presented themselves.

The problem with these oversimplified narratives, with their exclusive focus on the amazing deed, is that they make heroism seem irrelevant in our ordinary lives. As a pastime, we may daydream about what we might have done in similarly extraordinary situations, but we seldom let ourselves be truly affected by the heroes' examples and sacrifices. Drastically separating our lives from the realm of heroism, we risk falling back on reassuring and numbing narratives about our smallness and ordinariness. If instead we approach heroes as symbols to live by, their lives become a source of ongoing inspiration. And heroic figures—mythological or otherwise—then appear in our fantasies and nighttime dreams, forcing us to recognize qualities in ourselves, like perseverance and courage, that we may be unaware of. This is the painstaking work of cultivating our character that prepares us for the challenges we will be called to face.

The treatment of Rosa Parks as an American icon is an example of the flattening of narratives about heroism. She is often celebrated as the quiet, well-mannered, Southern seamstress who refused to give up her bus seat for a white man in segregated Montgomery, Alabama, and who—with her singular act—ignited the civil rights movement in the 1950s. A much repeated trope is that "she was tired, so she sat down." As her biographer Jeanne Theoharis wrote, "the fable of Parks ... had become a national redemption story and cornerstone to the idea of a postracial America. This framing was appealing—simultaneously sober about the history of racism, lionizing of black courage, celebratory of American progress, and slippery in masking current inequities."[6] Parks herself dismissed such tamed narrative:

> People always say that I didn't give up my seat because I was tired, but that isn't true. I was not tired physically, or no more tired than I usually was at the end of a working day. I was not old, although some people have an image of me as being old then. I was forty-two. No, the only tired I was, was tired of giving in.[7]

Far from being quiet or meek, Parks had "a life history of being rebellious," as she herself remarked.[8] At a young age, she was well aware of racial oppression and injustice—"By the time I was six," she wrote in her autobiography, "I was old enough to realize that we were actually not free."[9] Because terrorist organizations were targeting black communities with church burnings, beatings, and killings, her grandfather kept a shotgun close by in their house. He would say, "I don't know how long I would last if they came breaking in here, but I'm getting the first one who comes through the door."[10] And as a child, Rosa Parks absorbed the tension of her time—"I remember thinking that whatever happened, I wanted to see it," she wrote, "I wanted to see him shoot that gun."[11]

She channeled her awareness of inequities by growing into a social activist. Together with many other black men and women, she joined in voter registration efforts, labor organizing, and fair trial rights. She was an active member of the National Association for the Advancement of Colored People (NAACP), for which she documented cases of racial discrimination, police brutality, and violence. She protested "colored" bathrooms and drank from "white" fountains.[12] She fully dedicated her life to the ambitious goal of achieving equality; hers was a Sisyphean toil, because she did not accept her current reality as the seawall on which grandiose visions break. And for her goal, she sacrificed the comfort and safety of a tamer life.

It is from this commitment to her cause that her celebrated act emerged. "It was very humiliating having to suffer the indignity of riding segregated buses twice a day, five days a week, to go downtown and work for white people," Parks recalled.[13] On December 1, 1955, Parks refused to relinquish her seat in the "colored section" to a white passenger and so was arrested. On the day of her trial, the Montgomery bus boycott started, organized by many community leaders including Reverend Martin Luther King Jr. To their own surprise, their efforts were successful in mobilizing the wider black community, whose vigorous response sustained the boycott for more than a year, until the Supreme Court struck down segregation.

Thinking back to her heroic act of defiance, Parks shared that she had not intended to be arrested or become a plaintiff to challenge the legal status of segregation. "I did not think about that at all. In fact if I had let myself think too deeply about what might happen to me, I might have gotten off the bus. But I chose to remain."[14] She was presented with an opportunity to personally do something that she had been hoping others would do. Biographer Theoharis so concluded:

> Rosa Parks was an experienced political organizer; [however,] ... there is no evidence of any sort of plan, no indication till the moment presented itself that Parks knew she could summon the courage to refuse to move from her seat. It is likely that she, like many black Montgomerians ... had thought and talked about what she would do if she were asked to give up her seat to a white person. But thinking or even talking about it and actually being able to act in the moment are vastly different.[15]

That is the difference between idle fantasy and actual engagement, and Parks chose the latter. Her heroic deed was the result of years of indignities, her racial and political awareness, the integrity of her character, and the readiness of the community around her. To focus only on the singular act is to overlook her toil as a citizen committed to justice and would miss the depth of her callings. In fact, Parks also credited her Christian faith as a source of inspiration: "From my upbringing and the Bible, I learned people should stand up for rights just as the children of Israel stood up to the Pharaoh."[16]

The Exodus narrative, indeed, has stirred the imagination of generations of reformers and revolutionaries, from the English republic of Oliver Cromwell to liberation theology in South America, from the American Revolution to Martin Luther King Jr. And it is with this last story that I end this chapter. A people enslaved in Egypt—the Israelites—found in Moses a leader to bring them from bondage to the promised land of freedom. At one harrowing juncture of their escape, chased by the Egyptian chariots, the Israelites were told by their God to push toward the Sea of Reeds: the waters would part, so they could walk across the sea to safety. And hence Moses, confident in this prophecy, led them to the seashore.

The hero I want to discuss here is actually not Moses. It is instead a young man, Nahshon, son of Amminadab. His name foretold his calling—Nahshon is taken to mean "stormy sea waves." He is mentioned in a rabbinical story describing a moment of hesitation by the Israelites at the shore of the Sea of Reeds.[17] The sea was stormy and deep—and it was not parting. When was the miracle going to happen? Was the sea going to split at all? The various tribes began arguing about what to do, and who should go in first. Moses himself became unsure of his plan and his leadership; he moved to the side and started praying. Sometimes, we need to take the first step in; then, the rest of the story unfolds on its own. The hero of this story, Nahshon, simply started to walk, by himself, into the sea. "Deliver me, O God, for the waters have reached my neck. I am sinking into the slimy deep and find no foothold," he cried out, "Let the floodwaters not sweep me away. Let the deep not swallow me."[18] It was only then that the sea parted for all to cross.

It is just as scary to enter the muddy waters of the unconscious, to be called to explore our own depths. Describing his own experiences, Carl Jung wrote:

> In order to grasp the fantasies which were stirring in me "underground," I knew that I had to let myself plummet down into them, as it were. I felt not only violent resistance to this, but a distinct fear. For I was afraid of losing command of myself and becoming a prey to the fantasies—and as a psychiatrist I realized only too well what that meant. After prolonged hesitation, however, I saw that there was no other way out. I had to take the chance, had to try to gain power over them; for I realized that if I did not do so, I ran the risk of their gaining power over me. A cogent motive for my making the attempt was the conviction that I could not expect of my patients something I did not dare to do myself.[19]

With similar integrity and courage, we too can engage with our fantasies and nighttime dreams, investigate our motivations, work on our anger and fears, embrace our hurt, face our compulsions and addictions, and even attempt to change our personality—these all being grandiose and heroic endeavors. These private efforts may never be publicly recognized; after all, there has always been unsung heroism. However, we may find consolation in knowing that we are living true to our callings.

Notes

1. Sullenberger, *Sully*, 156.
2. Sullenberger, *Sully*, 211. All in italics in the original.
3. Sullenberger, "Flight 1549."
4. Sullenberger, *Sully*, 292.
5. Sullenberger, "Flight 1549."
6. Theoharis, *Rosa Parks*, viii.
7. Parks, *My Story*, 116.
8. As cited in Theoharis, *Rosa Parks*, 1.
9. Parks, *My Story*, 30.
10. Parks, *My Story*, 30.
11. Parks, *My Story*, 31.
12. See Theoharis, *Rosa Parks*, 68.
13. Parks, *My Story*, 109.
14. Parks, *My Story*, 116.
15. Theoharis, *Rosa Parks*, 67.
16. Brinkley, *Rosa Parks*, 14–5.
17. Sotah 37a.
18. Psalm 69:2–16. *Tanakh: A New Translation of the Holy Scriptures According to the Traditional Hebrew Text* (Philadelphia: Jewish Publication Society, 1985).
19. Jung, *Memories, Dreams, Reflections*, 178.

References

Brinkley, D. *Rosa Parks: A Life*. New York City: Penguin, 2000.
Jung, C. G. *Memories, Dreams, Reflections*. New York: Random House, 1989. First published 1961.
Parks, R. *My Story*. With Jim Haskins. New York: Penguin, 1992.
Sullenberger, C. B. "Flight 1549: Saving 155 Souls in Minutes." Interview by Katie Couric, *60 Minutes*, CBS, February 8, 2009.
Sullenberger, C. B. *Sully: My Search for What Really Matters*. With Jeffrey Zaslow. New York: William Morrow, 2016.
Theoharis, J. *The Rebellious Life of Mrs. Rosa Parks*. Boston: Beacon Press, 2013.

14

WISDOM AND THE ACCEPTANCE OF OUR INSIGNIFICANCE

"...but I felt very awkward that my joke wasn't funny." These were frequent remarks in the nighttime dreams of a young man I worked with. He came to therapy because he felt numb and unhappy. Having recently moved to Chicago, he had met some new people but did not feel close to anyone in particular—things just did not seem to click, leaving him lonely. There were no other obvious difficulties in his present life, yet he felt lost and directionless. As we talked, it became clear to us both that these somber feelings had been present for a long time. Only a liberal use of recreational drugs had created some peaks of excitement, although always followed by deep valleys of bad moods.

Being as engaged in therapy as he was, he shared stories—stories from his past that had never been told in such honest detail before. For instance, he shared that he had struggled committing to a career, always unsure about his worth in any field. He spoke of fantasies of success, of becoming wildly rich via trading; but these fantasies were not joyful, they had no life to them. He told me about his romantic relationships, and how over the years he had come not to expect much in terms of mutual love or support from his partners. He recalled his earliest memories, all the way back to his sense of not having been wished into life—as a toddler, he had been placed up for adoption, unlike his siblings who stayed with his biological mother. The feeling of being unwanted and unloved had extended to his adoptive family too, from whom he had largely estranged himself.

These backward-looking explorations into his life experiences, aided by his many dreams guiding our conversations, did not last forever. New perspectives soon emerged. For instance, he came to realize that his adoptive family was neurotic—as all families are—but also loving. He began to look at the ways he pushed people away, missing out on opportunities for connection. He explored his fantasies, including those grandiose fantasies that had long been buried under all these wounds, misunderstandings, and confusion. As therapy progressed, the veil of numbness lifted, and he felt a renewed desire for life. At that time, he shared the following dream:

> I was at the "L" train station. Some kids were hopping the fence to get in, and I looked at them disdainfully as they broke the rules. I wondered why they were doing that. I got on the train, but the tracks suddenly ended, and our train turned into a floating pirate ship. The next thing I knew, I was going through the ocean, or the rainforest, in a sort of real-life obstacle course. I was surrounded by a bunch of eight- to twelve-year-old boys, and I was like their camp counselor.
>
> We were having a great time but knew it was actually a little dangerous since it was in the wild. A bear trap snapped shut on my foot, but luckily it was old, did not really work, and only cut my skin very slightly. I felt very fortunate that it was not a bad cut. I got out and looked over, and one of the younger kids had an arrowhead stuck in his foot, but he too only had a very slight cut. I asked if he wanted me to pull it out, and he said yes, so I did.
>
> Parents began calling for us to stop playing and come inside. The rainforest became an indoor gym, where we continued the obstacle course. There were lots of gymnastics coaches watching, and the kids' parents were also watching from the outside. I helped the kids play and have fun until they slowly got done and went to their parents.
>
> I felt it was my chance to impress the gymnastics coaches, so I began doing lots of backflips and good landings on this gymnastics obstacle course thing. I was surprised to find out that I was that good. I was very impressed with myself and felt proud.

My patient did not go on to become a camp counselor, nor did he start doing gymnastics. Instead, we understood the dream's exciting imagery as energy arising from grandiose fantasies. For instance, he felt stronger and less concerned about being wounded by life—in the dream, he easily dealt with the bear trap and the arrow. He realized that when his mood lifted, his daily life in Chicago could be adventurous—like a playful obstacle course—without having to resort to "fun rides" induced by drugs. He also became comfortable being a little exhibitionistic, to lightheartedly show off his abilities.

It would have been a mistake to suggest that his fantasies were childish; it would have robbed him of his growing vitality. Instead, through these grandiose imaginings, he started to feel more confident that he had something valuable to offer and that he was worthy of having been born. Over time, he was able to channel this energy in meaningful ways in his daily life. He was more social and open with people and started dating. He felt good about himself, a feeling he had not experienced before.

This is the vitality that is lost when we ignore our unconscious fantasies. Shunning our expansive emotions and intuitions in favor of the safety of the familiar, proper, and conventional, we stifle our lives. But if we explore our grandiose fantasies and engage with our callings, then we receive—as if a gift—the felt sense that we matter and that our lives matter. We become empowered to believe that our choices make a difference.

And yet, we would be too self-assured if we were to claim that our choices make *all* the difference. The ego, of course, likes to think that is the case, that we are fully in control of our destiny. The truth is that our lives unfold in ways that are mostly beyond our control. We can strive for self-awareness and introspection. We can commit to our callings and put forward our best efforts. However, succeeding in our pursuits is not always in the cards.

This was a recurrent theme in the work of the poet Robert Frost. Over the course of his life, Frost was hailed as "a poet first of all of the American character," as *Time* magazine wrote in 1923. The identification of his poetry with the character of his nation mainly rested on the centrality of choice, individualism, and freedom.[1] His poem "The Road Not Taken" is widely popular in the United States and beyond. At a crossroads in the woods (and figuratively, in life), the narrator was confronted by two possible paths and had to pick one over the other.[2] The author David Orr wrote, "As the ninety thousandth high school valedictorian declaims the poem's final stanza"—where the narrator says he picked the road less traveled, a distinctive choice that seems to have made *all* the difference in his life—"everyone in the audience understands that they are being encouraged not simply to continue picking less traveled roads, but to aspire to a certain kind of glorified personhood."[3] Indeed the poem, often mistitled as "The Road Less Traveled," is most commonly interpreted as a celebration of the individual spirit, risk-taking, and the importance of choosing one's own destiny. Orr and scholars before him, however, argued that Frost intentionally built more than one perspective into his poem.

The story goes that Frost was inspired to write "The Road Not Taken" to tease a friend, the British poet Edward Thomas. Together, they used to go for long walks in the English countryside, talking about literature and life. Apparently, whenever Thomas led them down a path, he would often come to regret the choice, wondering about the scenery they might have missed by not going some other way. It is as a playful commentary on these countryside regrets that Frost wrote his celebrated poem. And if we do a close reading, we realize that the two roads described were not all that different; the narrator observes they were equally worn, suggesting people regularly walked along them both.

Yet, by the end of the poem, the narrator describes the road he chose as the less popular one, that is the unconventional choice—a clear contradiction that many readers miss. Hence, this is a poem that "almost everyone gets wrong," quipped Orr.[4] Rather than an exaltation of individuality and choice, it seems that Frost offered a critique on the self-congratulatory stories and retrospective narratives that we tell about our lives. In thinking that it was really our choices that made all the difference, we end up taking excessive credit for our achievements. The reverse is also true: sometimes we assume too much responsibility for our failures, leading to feelings of shame.[5] In either case, whether we succeed or fail, our desire for control makes us interpret everything as if it uniquely resulted from our choices and efforts—the ego tends to overestimate its powers.

There are at least two factors that conspire to thwart our best-laid plans—two factors that trump our will and egos. The first is the relentless influence of the unconscious, those motivations and callings that pull us away from our superficially-chosen pursuits. At a time when he doubted his decision to pursue a doctoral program in physics, a friend of mine decided that he wanted to become a business consultant and finally make good money. He had been feeling overwhelmed by the years of study still ahead and the uncertainties of an academic career. But he loved physics! Having applied to consulting positions, he was called by a firm for an interview. The first step of their selection process was a math test—something my friend clearly excelled in. Yet, he utterly failed it, effectively ending his consulting career before it started. He shared with me that, no matter how hard he tried to solve those math questions, he just could not understand what was being asked. While taking the test, he had a feeling of unreality, even wondering if the test was actually impossible, and some sort of prank was being played on him. It was as if something inside had sabotaged his ability to focus and do math, leaving him in a haze. When the ego sets sail away from our own callings, the unconscious may prevent the flight—at least until there is some reckoning and compromise.

Alignment with the unconscious, of course, does not prevent all failures in life. Even when we are clear about our callings, we may never accomplish our sought-after goals. For instance, our research ideas may not come to fruition, our artistic endeavors may fail to be recognized, or our family planning may not pan out as wished. This is because of the sheer randomness of life, the second factor that all too often thwarts the ego's plans. The Greeks acknowledged this intrinsic randomness when they placed Chaos first in their creation myth. Before all the gods and humans were born, even before Earth existed, there was already Chaos, a murky and shapeless mass of ill-assorted elements that was also thought of as the deep chasm—a chasm that remains at the foundation of our existence.[6]

I am not sharing the story of Chaos to argue that life truly is "random," that no deeper meaning or higher power exists beneath it all—I leave that metaphysical question to our own religious feelings and beliefs. What I suggest is that it is grandiose and narcissistic for anyone to claim to know the ultimate meaning of everything, including the most tragic and absurd events in the lives of others. For some, there is always a clear religious explanation that they feel compelled to pedantically share. Others instead point out the workings of psychological, unconscious factors; for instance, they may say that a business venture was doomed to fail because of *hubris*, because the entrepreneur was too arrogant—forgetting that after the fact, we all are accurate fortune-tellers. Such tightly held certainties betray a desire to control the unintelligible, the "murky abyss." These fantasies are an ego trip that most often results in a heartless—and so inhuman—worldview.

By acknowledging instead that life is shaped by the unconscious and by chance events, the ego is relativized. In his analysis of "The Road Not Taken," Orr concluded:

> [Different worldviews] emerge in the uncertain ground between the poem's popular interpretation and its more critically acceptable reading. The former imagines [an ego] ... that has chosen the less traveled road to emerge in its full splendor. The latter presupposes [an ego] ... that is unsure of its own choices, aware of its tendency to invent explanations for events over which it has no control, and skeptical of its future stability.[7]

And it is an achievement to be able to embrace forces beyond our control, doubts about our choices, and perspectives alternative to ours. It is to know that we are not always right and that we do not always get what we want. That is how we grow to accept our insignificance—our limitations, weaknesses, and inevitable failures—a sobering feeling indeed.

I find it fascinating that some of the most poignant reflections on our insignificance have emerged from one of the grandest endeavors of the human species: space exploration. The Voyager 1 spacecraft is currently the human-made object furthest away from Earth. Launched in 1977, its initial mission included flybys of Jupiter and Saturn. It is now 22 billion kilometers (14 billion miles) away from Earth, having left the solar system and reached interstellar space. It is still working and transmitting data. In 1990, as suggested by the astronomer Carl Sagan, NASA had Voyager 1 turn its camera toward Earth and take a picture of our planet from the outskirts of the solar system. Taken from that distance, Earth appears in the picture as a small point of light, a "pale blue dot" in a sea of darkness. Sagan commented:

> Look again at that dot. That's here. That's home. That's us. On it everyone you love, everyone you know, everyone you ever heard of, every human being who ever was, lived out their lives. The aggregate of our joy and suffering, thousands of confident religions, ideologies, and economic doctrines, every hunter and forager, every hero and coward, every creator and destroyer of civilization, every king and peasant, every young couple in love, every mother and father, hopeful child, inventor and explorer, every teacher of morals, every corrupt politician, every "superstar," every "supreme leader," every saint and sinner in the history of our species lived there—on a mote of dust ... The Earth is a very small stage in a vast cosmic arena.[8]

Whenever we are reminded of the scale of things, how can we not doubt—even for just a moment—our most tightly held convictions and grand pursuits?

The vertigo of looking into the cosmic abyss of space—or of thinking about our own mortality, as I had to do when I volunteered in home hospice—gives us an opportunity to pause and wonder about what we are striving for.

It is at these times that we open up to the experience of wisdom. Wisdom results from our ability to hold true two opposing ideas at once. On one hand, we practice acceptance of our own insignificance, which keeps us sane and grounded, preventing us from becoming inflated beyond measure or feeling responsible for everything. On the other hand, we embrace our grandiosity, which infuses our lives with a sense of possibilities and hope for what is or might become.

By embracing this tension between insignificance and grandiosity, we can strive to "forge an ego that does not break down when incomprehensible things happen," as Carl Jung wrote, "an ego that endures, that endures the truth, and that is capable of coping with the world and with fate. Then, to experience defeat is also to experience victory. Nothing is disturbed—neither inwardly nor outwardly, for one's own continuity has withstood the current of life and of time."[9] When we abstain from empty pursuits, engage with our callings, survive our inevitable share of failures, and still manage not to become cynical or defeated, then we experience wisdom as the ability to rise above these cycles of gains and losses.

I had my moment of wisdom at a time when it seemed I would not be able to establish myself in the United States, a goal for which I had sacrificed much. This was years ago, when—struggling to find a job and unsure if I could maintain my immigration status—I had to face the possibility of returning to Italy without being able to practice psychology there, leaving me with little to show for all my efforts. Yet, in the midst of this impending crisis, I dreamt that I was back in Italy eating a delicious pizza, made with *real* mozzarella. Upon waking up, I thought that even in the face of failure, there is something to look forward to—a thought that brought a smile and relief, as I kept looking for a job against the upcoming deadline.

Humor is surely an expression of wisdom, as it compassionately deflates the puffed-up ego—that hot-air balloon—by putting things into perspective. With humor, we can acknowledge our grandiose motivations without shame. After discussing for months how he was tired, had no time for himself, and wanted to work less, a patient of mine came to his session sharing that another opportunity had presented itself; he could open yet another restaurant. "Maybe I will do it just one more time," he said mischievously. Feeling his excitement but also remembering his exhaustion, I could not help but say, "maybe one day *all* restaurants in Chicago will be yours!"—to which we both burst into laughter.[10]

♦

With her retirement approaching and a gnawing sense of confusion and emptiness, a woman came to therapy feeling her life had been a series of disconnected events. From an adventurous beginning—teaching English in a foreign country, falling in love there and having a daughter with a local, and later pursuing an ultimately successful academic career—she also faced a series of upsetting developments—a divorce, effectively being a single parent, years of conflict with her now-adult daughter, and the difficulties of acculturating back to the United States. Over the years, these successes and challenges alternated one after another—not an unusual life trajectory—but she wondered what it all summed up to be.

Through her work in therapy, she uncovered that the series of choices, accidents, and twists and turns in her life was not as fragmented as she had felt; instead, she started believing that even the difficult times had turned out to be opportunities for appreciating her resilience, reevaluating her usual assumptions, and taking risks in new directions. It is by observing the cycles of victories and defeats that we learn what persists and what instead is fleeting in ourselves. In her case, she realized how her life had been shaped by her endless curiosity and her striving for absolute self-reliance.

Around that time, she decided to sign up for a yoga retreat. Initially uncomfortable opening up, she soon relaxed into connecting with the other participants, all women younger than her. Each of them reminded my patient of herself at an earlier time in her own life. For instance, the youngest participant was restless, unsure about what she wanted—it was her fourth retreat in a year; maybe she could become a yoga teacher, or perhaps something else. Another participant had just met a professional musician on a weekend trip, whom she described as an amazing man. She was now texting endlessly with him—sometimes even during the yoga sessions—and my patient could imagine the woman chasing him across the globe. Lastly, another woman had signed up for the retreat because she experienced burnout while writing a book. She was an academician like my patient and very ambitious; her marriage was crumbling, but she mostly spoke of her career.

My patient saw—as if from the outside looking in—the grandiose fantasies and strivings of her own past. She knew how exciting these endeavors can feel, but also where they might lead, and what obstacles those women could soon encounter. Most importantly, she observed the other women without judging them or herself. Instead, she described the yoga retreat to me with humor and empathy—the wisdom of having lived and learned. As she spoke of her pleasant experience, I thought of the novella *A Christmas Carol* by Charles Dickens. Like in that classic story, each woman at the yoga retreat was a visitor who brought my patient more clarity about herself. With this growing acceptance of her life's course, her anxiety that she did not live "properly" was allayed. She was able to try and embrace the next chapter in her life with renewed energy and confidence.

Living in the space between insignificance and grandiosity, hard realities and creatively imagined possibilities, factors outside of our control and the necessity to engage with our callings, we can strive to develop our awareness and character. While our grandiosity has the potential to wreak havoc on our lives and on our communities, it is my belief that, when approached with doubt, humor, integrity, and wisdom, grandiosity can have a positive and transformative effect on us and the world.

I close with another creation story—this time from the Jewish tradition—that says that when the earth was initially formed, its Maker deemed the overall project incomplete. To finish what had been started required the active participation of humans. In this narrative, people are still participating in the unfolding of the grand story of creation with their individual actions—they collaborate with their Maker. Unfortunately, that we may contribute to such a vast endeavor is mostly visible in the negative nowadays. We have the capacity to destroy humanity and the whole planet with our choices, whether through nuclear weapons or our indolence about the environmental crisis—the folly of war and our reckless dominion over nature are the result of destructive grandiose fantasies left untamed. This Jewish story, however, has a hopeful side too. Each of us can strive to channel our passions and ambitions to contribute to the sanity and wellbeing of the world. Filled with a sense of purpose and courage—and each in our own way—we can have an impact larger than our individual selves. Hasidic Rabbi Simcha Bunim of Peshischa suggested people always carry two pieces of paper, one in each pocket.[11] When inflated by grandiosity, we can reach out for the one that says, "I am dust and ashes." When struggling to find hope to continue, we can instead pull out the one that says, "The world was created for me." For Rabbi Bunim, both statements were equally true; may we too be reminded of both perspectives always.

Notes

1. See Orr, *Road Not Taken*.
2. For conciseness, I refer to the narrator with he/his/him.
3. Orr, *Road Not Taken*, 134.
4. Orr, *Road Not Taken*, 7. Even Frost's friend initially missed the subtlety. In a letter, Frost explained the poem's inside joke to him, causing Thomas to reply, "I doubt if you can get anybody to see the fun of the thing without showing them & advising them which kind of laugh they are to turn on." As quoted by Orr, *Road Not Taken*, 67.
5. Shame emerges when we take all the responsibility for our failures, making failures into a reflection of our character and worth.
6. The use of "chaos" to signify disorder and confusion is more recent but clearly related to its original mythological meaning.
7. Orr, *Road Not Taken*, 140. Orr used the word "self," which I replaced with "ego" for consistency with the use of both words in this book.
8. Sagan, *Pale Blue Dot*, 6.
9. Jung, *Memories, Dreams, Reflections*, 297.
10. Heinz Kohut argued that grandiosity can become "gradually integrated into the web of our ego as a healthy enjoyment of our own activities and successes and as an adaptively useful sense of disappointment tinged with anger and shame over our failures and shortcomings." Kohut, "Forms and Transformations of Narcissism," in Morrison, *Essential Papers on Narcissism*, 70. In that article, he described five qualities that originate from grandiosity: creativity, empathy, acceptance of transience and mortality, humor, and wisdom. Kohut used the terms "narcissism" and "grandiosity" differently than I, as discussed in chapter 7, and here I favor consistency with the terminology of this book.
11. Buber, *Tales of the Hasidim*, 249–50.

References

Buber, M. *Tales of the Hasidim*. New York: Schocken Books, 1991. First published 1947.

Jung, C. G. *Memories, Dreams, Reflections*. New York: Random House, 1989. First published 1961.

Morrison, A. P., ed. *Essential Papers on Narcissism*. New York: New York University Press, 1986.

Orr, D. *The Road Not Taken: Finding America in the Poem Everyone Loves and Almost Everyone Gets Wrong*. New York: Penguin Press, 2015.

Sagan, C. *Pale Blue Dot: A Vision of the Human Future in Space*. New York: Ballantine Books, 1994.

15

THE GOAL IS TO FIND GOLD

"Grant that whatever my person touches be turned to yellow gold!"[1] Having generously attended to the god Bacchus' senile mentor, King Midas was granted a wish as a reward. His request for the riches of gold, however, was excessive. Midas' "golden touch," as it has come to be known, brought unintended, destructive consequences upon him—a reminder that we should be careful what we wish for. Throughout this book, we have explored how grandiosity can manifest in so many different ways, such as dreams of fame, knowledge, beauty, perfection, morality, and victimhood. Yet, I suspect that of all these possible fantasies and strivings, we will always associate grandiosity first and foremost with dreams of wealth and riches, that is with the pursuit of gold.

One of the seven metals known since antiquity, gold has risen to a central place in our imagination and fantasies. It appears in fairy tales, mythologies, and religions across cultures and eras, and it continues to show up in our nighttime dreams. Surely, the evocative powers of the shiny metal are rooted in its chemical properties—its resistance to corrosion and oxidation—and its market value—it used to be the most expensive among the metals. But psychologically, gold is above all a powerful symbol of grandiose endeavors, even in our time of online bank statements, credit cards, and digital currencies.

As always, the risk is that we take the symbols and fantasies springing up from our unconscious, including our wish for gold, too concretely—in Latin *concretus* means thick, hardened, and solidified. This was undoubtedly Midas' case, as his fantasy became way too concrete. Having had his wish granted, everything Midas touched turned instantly into hard gold: a twig, a stone, a clod of earth, and even the columns of his house. He was elated. "He dreamed of everything turned to gold, and his hopes soared beyond the limits of his imagination."[2] That is, until it was time for dinner.

> Servants set before him tables piled high with meats, and with bread in abundance. But then, when he touched a piece of bread, it grew stiff and hard: if he hungrily tried to bite into the meat, a sheet of gold encased the food, as soon as his teeth came in contact with it. He took some wine … the liquid could be seen turning to molten gold as it passed his lips.
>
> Wretched in spite of his riches, dismayed by the strange disaster which had befallen him, Midas prayed for a way to escape from his wealth, loathing what he had lately desired … the gold he now hated.[3]

Because Bacchus took pity on him, Midas was allowed to lose his nefarious "touch" by submerging himself in the Pactolus River, causing its riverbed to be scattered with gold nuggets. In antiquity, in fact, the Pactolus was known to contain gold in its sands.

We too can just as concretely pursue the fantasies that stir us up. Our tendency toward literalism shows just how unfamiliar we have become with our inner, symbolic life. Dreams at night and fantasies by day spring up from the unconscious in a language that is rich in striking images, grand visions, and intense emotions. We so easily dismiss these products of our imagination as childish and silly. Yet we do not realize that we are actually caught in these fantasies, so much so that we are concretely pursuing them. If instead we became more familiar with the existence of such symbolic life and knew how to relate to it, we might be freed from compulsively enacting it.

A young man I worked with—just about to graduate college—was discussing his plans for the future. He said to me that his first task for life after graduation was finding a job that pays well, by which he meant a consulting job that pays *a lot*. I asked him, "What do you need that money for?" "To save it," he said. "Save it for what?" I wondered aloud. "Well, so that I can invest it." "What will you do with all your investments?" Long pause. "Maybe… maybe one day I will buy a motorboat." Finally, there was something real. The problem was that he did not really enjoy boating; he had not done much of it either. He just thought he would like having a boat, he explained as I inquired more, because he imagined it filled with friends sharing drinks and food.

This young man had not sought friendships in college, as he thought that to be professionally successful he had to always be focused, studious, and ambitious. And, of course, one does not need a motorboat to make friends and hang out with them, although it is surely lovely to be out on the water in good company. With further exploration and introspection, his dreams of wealth could have transformed into something potentially more fulfilling—for instance, if he attended more directly to his desire to be part of a community. For the time being, wealth was his pursuit—he was looking for gold.

To better understand the psychological power of gold as a symbol, we can turn to an unlikely place: alchemy. While later it became known as the Noble Art, alchemy may have begun as recipes to counterfeit metals. In third-century CE Byzantine Egypt, people were recording chemical procedures to color cheap metals so that they would look like silver and gold—clearly a scam. But from these origins, alchemy developed into a complex system of knowledge that linked experimental research with (highly imaginative) speculations about nature, philosophy, and religion.[4]

Not many people know, for instance, that among its practitioners there were numerous forefathers of modern science. For instance, Isaac Newton—renowned for his insights on gravitation, the nature of light, and calculus—spent countless hours studying alchemical books and trying alchemical procedures in his laboratory. However, Newton mostly hid these interests from his contemporaries. And for centuries, his biographers did not publicize his alchemical work either, fearing that his reputation would be damaged. After all, throughout the thousand-plus years it was actively practiced—from antiquity to medieval times, and then again during the Renaissance—alchemy experienced alternating fortunes and a dubious reputation, often regarded as a hoax, a magic practice, or a pseudo-science.

Together with its origin in counterfeiting, the negative assessment of alchemy has derived from its obscure language rich in mythological and religious references. In fact, in addition to familiar substances like sulfur, mercury, or silver, alchemical books refer to abstruse things like the fiery dragon, the doves of Diana, or the eagles of Mercury. The texts present obscure instructions on how to purify, combine, and transform these substances, while also specifying that the outcome of the procedures depends on the motivations of the practicing alchemist. Only those with the right religious attitude could successfully approach the Noble Art, we are told. And so, we are left wondering if alchemists were discussing actual workshop procedures, similar to those performed in chemistry labs, or something different altogether.

As a child, I must have been inspired by alchemy when I spent countless hours at the sink in my home, combining soaps, hair products, and a favorite green apple perfume. I would then transfer the mixtures into a collection of containers and spray bottles, through filters made of paper towels. When I was a little older, I graduated to boiling vinegar in the kitchen to examine the residual dry powder. (While writing this book, I found out that it was actually a dangerous thing to do.) My mother used to say I was doing *i pasticci,* "the messes." I vividly remember those many hours immersed in play as immensely exciting, filled as they were with imaginary discoveries and accomplishments.

But while I had no idea what I was doing, historians have recently dispelled many of the misperceptions surrounding alchemy. There has been a rehabilitation of alchemy within the history of science, and alchemy has been shown to be not a curious eccentricity, but the work of "serious thinkers and talented experimentalists," experimentalists who were steeped in the understanding of nature of their time, including the early chemical and metallurgical knowledge.[5]

For instance, armed with knowledge of both chemistry and mythology, the historian Lawrence Principe was able to make sense of obscure alchemical passages. When working with instructions like, "Introduce to the eagle the old dragon who has dwelt long among the rocks, ... and set the two upon a hellish seat, then Pluto will blow strongly and drive out from the cold dragon a flying, fiery spirit whose great heat will burn up the feathers of the eagle," Principe convincingly argues that the eagle is ammonium chloride, the dragon is potassium nitrate, and Pluto—the god of Hell—is simply some strong heat.[6] Because Principe is also a chemist, he tested his educated guesses in his laboratory, obtaining the fascinating results predicted by the alchemical text. Decoding their allegorical language, Principe showed that at least some alchemists were describing actual chemical procedures and had a remarkable knowledge of materials and chemical reactions.[7] Watching a video of Principe excitingly talk about his research made me think back to my excitement as a child with soaps and boiling vinegar—it is such a blessing to love one's own job.

But alchemy was not only chemical reactions. We know that any creative endeavor stirs the imagination and acquires meaning above and beyond the concrete. This is true for any scientific undertaking; for instance, as we discussed in the previous chapter, cosmic explorations have evoked rich reflections on human life. Likewise, in producing their allegorical narratives, alchemists embedded their work with ideas reflecting their worldview, spirituality, and personal searches for meaning. As Principe wrote,

> For the early modern thinker, such analogies—or metaphors, or harmonies, call them what you will—meant vastly more than they do to [us] moderns. For them, an analogy was something actually existing in the world—a real connection intentionally built into the fabric of what is, …[flowing] from their vision of a world created by a uniform, omnipotent, omniscient God; a world endowed in every corner with meaning, message, and purpose … Hence, observations of the natural world carried meanings far beyond the isolated literal object under immediate consideration.[8]

If we are raised in a secular culture, the religious worldview of alchemists may not resonate with us. Yet, when we pay attention to our nighttime dreams and their symbolic language, then all kinds of alchemical images, ancient notions, and religious themes come to life in our otherwise modern minds. This insight was the contribution of Carl Jung to the study of alchemy.

While Jung initially considered alchemy "off the beaten track and rather silly," he later came to believe that "the alchemists were talking in symbols" of spiritual and psychological transformation.[9] Alchemical books and theories, then, provided him with a rich repertoire of images and metaphors that proved helpful in better understanding the dreams of his patients. Curiously enough, one patient of Jung who famously had dreams rich with alchemical themes was the Nobel Prize-winning physicist Wolfgang Pauli, a pioneer of quantum theory.[10]

Alchemists held that one of their most important goals was the transformation of cheap materials into precious gold. Certainly, some may have been looking for real gold, for concrete ways to become rich. But many alchemists clearly said that they instead aimed at the discovery of what they called *aurum non vulgi*, "not the common gold," or *aurum philosophicum*, "philosophical gold." We do not know what alchemists were referring to when using these puzzling terms. Possibly, they were seeking a substance that only looks like gold, maybe even a counterfeited material. Alternatively, they might have been dealing in symbols: their special gold may not have been an actual substance, but something nevertheless very precious. After all, philosophical gold was also referred to as the giver of life, the substance that heals all illness, the philosopher's stone, the source of all knowledge, the Sun, and even the divinity. In alchemy, concrete endeavors and metaphorical pursuits are blurred together, and alchemical symbols emerge anew with the power to stir us.

Interpreted psychologically, philosophical gold represents what is most valuable in our lives and in ourselves, those commitments and insights that make us feel alive and with a sense of purpose. And when we live in pursuit of our callings, then we may discover that source of vitality within us that Jung called both the "center of the personality" and the "living gold."[11]

"A Gold Rush Revival in Italy, With Nuggets the Size of Bread Crumbs"—was the title of a recent article in *The New York Times*.[12] Apparently, nowadays searching for gold is a hobby with dedicated enthusiasts, a weekend activity that has generated organized clubs and competitions with thousands in attendance. For instance, near the Italian Alps, the Elvo River titillates amateur gold seekers with the occasional specks of gold, obtained after hours of sifting through its sands.

This naturally-occurring gold had already inspired the imagination of Primo Levi, a celebrated Italian author best known for his book *If This Is a Man*.[13] He was an Italian Jew and Holocaust survivor who wrote powerfully about what he personally witnessed during World War II. He was also a passionate chemist by trade. Another one of his books, *The Periodic Table*, has an alchemical flavor to it; every chapter is titled after a chemical element—Sulfur, Lead, Uranium—and narrates his experiences during the war and after his return to Italy. In the chapter "Gold," Levi wrote about his arrest by the Fascist militia after the armistice of September 8, 1943, and his time in prison in northern Italy, before he was sent to the Nazi concentration camps. While detained, he is told by a fellow prisoner about a nearby river that carries gold in its sands. The gold is not just everywhere: it is in some particular bends of the river that happen to be well hidden and off the beaten track. The location of these prolific bends is a secret transmitted through the generations, from parent to child. Levi's prison mate, who does "many different kinds of work," including dabbling in contraband, tells him that he "wouldn't change places with a banker" because his gold means freedom.

> You see, it's not that there is so much gold: there is in fact very little, you wash it for a whole night and you manage to get two or three grams out of it: but it never ends. You can go back when you wish: the next night or a

134 The courage of our insignificance

The completion of the work: The Sun of Perfection. (Illustration from *Splendor Solis*, 1582.)

month later, whenever you feel like it, and the gold has grown back; and it's that way forever and ever, like grass comes back in the fields. And so there are no people who are freer than us.[14]

Neither do our contemporary Italian gold-seekers become rich with their diligent and effortful work. Yet, they spend hours on their knees with their hands in the flow of the water, sifting through soil and pebbles—engaged and focused as they pursue their hobby. If material wealth is not their main motivation, I wonder if they are animated by the realization that gold is a symbol, and that their "living gold" is more important than wealth. When the prison mate finished sharing about his river, he suggested that maybe one day Levi, too, could try searching its sands for gold. Levi became lost in thoughts:

> Of course I would try it: What wouldn't I try? During those days, when I was waiting courageously enough for death, I harbored a piercing desire for everything, for all imaginable human experiences, and I cursed my previous life, which it seemed to me I had profited from little or badly, and I felt time running through my fingers ... Of course I would search for gold: not to get rich but to try out a new skill, to see again the earth, air, and water ... and to find again my chemical trade in its essential and primordial form ... precisely, the art of separating metal from gangue.[15]

One of the gold seekers interviewed for *The New York Times*'s article, Giorgio Bogni, is a geologist who loves to spend time visiting streams. "Gold panning is fun," he said, "it's a hobby, but it's also a form of meditation, in nature, with the sounds of the river around you." The question "Is That All There Is?" to a weekend by the river, looking at rocks and searching for gold, does not spoil his enthusiasm. "It's usually a grueling day's work," he shared, "and you come home and your wife looks at the two atoms you found and says, 'Is that all?' But I'm happy."[16]

Notes

1. Ovid, *Metamorphoses* 11.68ff. Translated by Mary M. Innes (London: Penguin Books, 1955).
2. Ovid, *Metamorphoses*, 11.106ff.
3. Ovid, *Metamorphoses*, 11.106ff.
4. An excellent and accessible exposition of the history and ideas of alchemy is Principe, *Secrets of Alchemy*.
5. Principe, *Secrets of Alchemy*, 170.
6. Principe, *Secrets of Alchemy*, 147. The text is from Basil Valentine, *Of the Great Stone*, 1:30–32. I am not able to do justice to Principe's delightful reconstructions with these few passages.
7. In light of these results, some of the Jungian interpretations of alchemical ideas and symbols may have to be revised or more tentatively stated. Some alchemists were current with the natural philosophies of their time, worked with actual chemical

reactions in their laboratories, and were purposely using code names to describe their work. While unconscious projection likely colored their choices of allegories and their understanding of the *opus*, it would be inaccurate to claim that all of alchemists' experiences are akin to dreams and visions. The possibility remains that at least some alchemists primarily described visions and unconscious fantasies, as customarily assumed by Jungian writers.

8. Principe, *Secrets of Alchemy*, 203–5. Elsewhere, Principe wrote that for some alchemists these analogies and metaphors "are neither arbitrary nor products of human imagination—they exist independently as real connections in the fabric of the world itself. They lie there hidden, waiting to be uncovered"— a description that brings to mind the idea of archetypes in Jungian psychology. Principe, *Secrets of Alchemy*, 201.
9. Jung, *Memories, Dreams, Reflections*, 204. It is worth noting that Principe and other modern historians of science—who generally are not keen on the importance of the unconscious and the symbolic life—tend to dismiss Jung's psychological approach to alchemy. Compare with Principe, *Secrets of Alchemy* 83–106.
10. An engaging account of Jung's work with Pauli is Miller, *137*.
11. Jung, *Mysterium Coniunctionis*, 263. This source of vitality and meaning is what Jung called "the Self."
12. Povoledo, "Gold Rush."
13. Published in English as Levi, *Survival in Auschwitz*.
14. Levi, *Periodic Table*, 136–7.
15. Levi, *Periodic Table*, 137.
16. Povoledo, "Gold Rush."

References

Jung, C. G. *Mysterium Coniunctionis*. Vol. 14 of *The Collected Works of C. G. Jung*, edited by H. Read, M. Fordham, G. Adler, and W. McGuire. Translated by R. F. C. Hull. Princeton, NJ: Princeton University Press, 1970.

Jung, C. G. *Memories, Dreams, Reflections*. New York: Random House, 1989. First published 1961.

Levi, P. *The Periodic Table*. Translated by Raymond Rosenthal. New York: Schocken Books, 1984.

Levi, P. *Survival in Auschwitz: The Nazi Assault on Humanity*. New York: Simon & Schuster, 1993. First published 1958.

Miller, A. I. *137: Jung, Pauli, and the Pursuit of a Scientific Obsession*. New York: W.W. Norton & Company, 2010.

Povoledo, E. "A Gold Rush Revival in Italy, with Nuggets the Size of Bread Crumbs," *New York Times*, June 28, 2017.

Principe, L. M. *The Secrets of Alchemy*. Chicago and London: The University of Chicago Press, 2013.

INDEX

Note: Page numbers followed by "*n*" indicate notes.

acceptance: of insignificance 119–126; of transience and mortality 126*n*10
aging 27–28, 33, 49
alchemy 130–131; as counterfeiting 131; Jungian interpretation of 136*n*11; rehabilitation of 131
altruism 63, 68, 78
Ananke 35
archetypes 10, 72*n*14
audience: and heroic feats 113; search for an 12, 49, 54
aurum non vulgi 132
aurum philosophicum 133

backward-looking fantasies 106
"Bartleby the Scrivener" 26
basic narcissistic mechanism 56
beauty 47–52
blissful state of infancy 7–8, 10
Botox 49

callings 77–78, 80; and dreams 97–98; and heroism 117; identifying 78, 91, 94; and introspection 95, 103; and romantic love 94
Calvino, Italo 86, 133–135
Captain Sully 113–115
Chaos 122
character: development of 114
children 7–13, 87; fantasies 7; neglect 11; psychology of 23
climbing 3–4, 105
conventional life 85, 120; and psychotherapy 96

corporate culture 34
cosmetics advertising 49
courage 78, 104; to abstain 103–110; to engage 113–118; of insignificance 104–105
creativity 87, 126*n*10
Crowhurst, Donald 39, 41, 43

da Morrone, Pietro 78–79
Dante: on Odysseus 41–42; on Pope Celestine 80, 84
dating 4, 26, 110, 120
de Saint-Exupéry, Antoine 18, 26–27
The Death of Ivan Ilyich 88–89, 114
delusions 71
desire for sameness 78; *see also* basic narcissistic mechanism
doubt 123; lack of 31, 40, 108
dreams 97; and alchemy 132; and anxiety 3; of being elected pope 98; and callings 97; of climbing 105; of Garden of Eden 106; of gold 129; Jungian interpretation of 105, 132; of love 110–111; of masks 109–110; of an obstacle course 120; of playing 120; of returning 124; of snake 106; of Trump xv

Echo 54
ego 8, 14*n*9, 56, 58, 121; development of 8, 14*n*12; ego complex 15*n*13; and inflation 70–71, 122; injuries to 11; values of 78
emerging adulthood 24

environmental crisis 126
eternal youth *see Puer Aeternus*
Exodus 117

Fabulous Fab 43
failure 34–35
fairy tales 47–49; the Grimms 47; and Jungian interpretations 48; "Snow White" 47–48
fame 39–45
family romances 87
fantasies of changing others 108
Fitzgerald, F. Scott 20
Frankenstein or the Modern Prometheus 44
Freud, Sigmund 7–8, 53, 87
Frost, Robert 121

Garden of Eden 14*n*11, 42, *107*, 108; in a dream 106
Gates, Bill 20
gold *32*, 129, 133; in alchemy 130, 133; "living gold" 133
Golden Globe race 39
golden touch 129
grandiosity 7–13, 17–19, 25, 33, 43, 93; in adults 17; and alcohol and drug use 50–51; and anxiety 3, 19, 32, 50; and beauty 48–49; and comparisons 18, 68; compulsions 19, 23, 31, 34; destructiveness 10, 15*n*14, 71; fantasies 10, 17, 20, 25, 49, 81, 115; and loss of hope 84–85; and money 27, 34, 40, 44–45, 129, 130; and morality/moralism 66–67; vs narcissism 57; and "negative" qualities 19; and nostalgia 106; obsessions 5–6, 19, 23; and parenthood 51–52; and playfulness 120; and progressive ideals 64–65; of psychotherapists 108; and relatedness 10; and sexuality 51; and shame 3, 20, 126*n*5; and work 26, 32, 34, 50, 105
The Great Gatsby 20, 25
greater good 63, 65
Greek mythology 9–10, 41, 122
Guggenbühl-Craig, Adolf 111*n*5

hate of difference 55–56, 60*n*25
heroes 9, 48, 115
heroism 113, 115
hubris 122
humility 68, 83–84; and shame 91
humor 124, 126*n*10

idealized parental imago 14*n*12
impossible goals 4, 35, 69, 92
indecisiveness 110

infancy 7–8; blissful state of 7–8, 10, 13*n*6
inflation 70 *see* grandiosity
inner questions 3–4, 89
insignificance 104; acceptance of 123; and hope 126
instant gratification 25
introspection 95–96
"Is That All There Is?" xiii

Jacoby, Mario 59*n*19
Jewish creation story 126
Jonah 77–78
journaling 94–95
Jung, Carl 9, 42–43, 124; on alchemy 132–133; on inflation 70–71; on psychotherapy 109; and the Self 136*n*11; and the source of vitality 133; on the unconscious 117
Jungian psychology 97–98

Kernberg, Otto 54
King Midas 103, 129–130
knowledge: pursuit of 41
Kohut, Heinz 11, 59*n*19, 126*n*10; grandiose self 14*n*12; idealized parental imago 14*n*12

La Divina Commedia 41–42, 80, 84
laziness 84–89
lifegiver 61*n*31
The Little Prince 18, 26–27
living gold 133
love 93–94, 110

Mallory, George 3
Marco Polo 86
Mayer, Marissa 33
Melville, Herman 26, 39, 52
Metamorphoses 23, 52, *53*
Midas Muffler 103
Millennials 12
Mirror 48–49, 58, 61*n*34; mirrored image 57; mirroring 11; mother's face 58
money 39–45
morality 65–68
mortality 5, 69–70, 98, 124
motivations 3, 78, 97, 104
Mount Everest 3
Mount Olympus 9, 20

Nahshon 117
narcissism 9, 53, 56, 59*n*19, 60*n*25; and chance 122; core of 55; vs grandiosity 57; and paranoia 60*n*27; primary narcissism 54, 59*n*19
Narcissus 52, 56

National Association for Advancement of Colored People (NAACP) 116
Neumann, Erich 8
Newton, Isaac 131
nighttime dreams 92, 97–98, 106, 115

oceanic feeling 71
Odysseus 41–43
Orr, David 121, 123

papacy 80; dreams of 98
parents 8; blaming 28, 57, 61n30; inner world of 87; and self-esteem 11
Parks, Rosa 115
perfectionism 4, 27, 33
The Periodic Table 133
Person, Ethel 94
persona 67
Peter Pan *see Puer Aeternus*
Petrarch 80–81
philosophical gold *see aurum philosophicum*
Pope Celestine 79
power naps 50
pride 11
primary narcissism 8, 59n19
Principe, Lawrence 131–132, 136n8
procrastination 110
Prometheus 9, 12, 13, 31
provisional life 27
psychotherapy 4, 28, 55, 60n24, 109, 119; and callings 96; for couples 57; and literalism 130; and victimhood 69
Puer Aeternus 23, 106
Puer type 23–28, 41, 45, 79, 92, 110; backward-looking fantasies 106; and commitment 24–25; and psychotherapy 28; role of fantasies 25–27; self-esteem 25

Rabbi Simcha Bunim 126
racism 65, 71n3
Raymond, Roy 44–45
reality: limitations of 8, 12, 24–25
reality principle 35
refusal of responsibilities 26–27
religions 83–84
"The Road Not Taken" 121–123
Rosenwald Fund 63
Rowling, J. K. 28, 34–35

sacrifices 81
Sagan, Carl 123
savior complex 27
search for meaning 86, 132–133
self-esteem 12; birth of 9–10; deflated 19; parents and 11
self-help books 85
sense of being 14n9
sense of "I" 14n9
sexuality 51
Siegel, Allen 11–12
Sisyphus 31
Sisyphus types 31–35, 42, 57, 92
"Snow White" fairy tale 47–48
social media 49–50
space exploration 123
stone: philosopher's 133; and Sisyphus 31
suicide 41, 45, 52–53
Swift, Jonathan 47, 50
symbolic life 130; and alchemy 132
Symington, Neville 57
syphilis 64

templates of grandiosity 88; depth of 88; parents as 87; variety of 88
Tolstoy, Leo 88
Trump, Donald xiii xv; and bankruptcies 34
Tuskegee Study 64–66, 71n3

unconscious 3, 58; exploring 117; thwarting plans 122
unconscious choice 57

validating experiences 11
victimhood 69–70
Victoria's Secret 44–45
vocation *see* callings
von Franz, Marie-Louise 23–24, 58, 110

well-being of mankind 63
West, Marcus 14n9, 55–56, 60n26
whirling banner 84
Winnicott, Donald 8, 58, 97
wisdom 124–125, 126n10; of insignificance 119–126
wounded healer 111n5

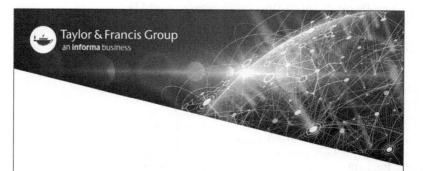